Kids and money: Fast track your kids for a practical life

Jordan Rivers

Published by A. I. Rivers, 2024.

KIDS AND MONEY: FAST TRACK YOUR KIDS FOR A PRACTICAL LIFE

First edition. July 29, 2024.

Copyright © 2024 Jordan Rivers.

ISBN: 979-8227082497

Written by Jordan Rivers.

Table of Contents

Kids and money: Fast-track your kids for a practical life

Introduction

When Sarah first attempted to explain the concept of money to her seven-year-old son, Tommy, she found herself stumbling over her words. "Money," she said, "is... well, it's what we use to buy things we need... and want." Tommy, wide-eyed, responded, "So, if I have enough money, can I buy every toy in the store?" Sarah chuckled, realizing this was just the beginning of many money conversations. This simple yet profound interaction underscores an essential truth: teaching kids about money is not just a responsibility—it's a necessity.

As the author of this book and a fervent advocate for practical financial education, I've dedicated myself to demystifying the world of money for the younger crowd. My journey into financial literacy began with a simple observation: too many adults struggle with money because they weren't taught the basics at a young age. Driven by a belief that understanding money is foundational to making wise financial decisions, I've crafted this book to serve as a bridge between financial concepts and young minds.

Our mission here is straightforward: to provide you, the adult in a child's life, with the tools and strategies necessary to teach kids aged 7 to 12 about money in a manner that is both engaging and simple. We'll bypass the complicated jargon and focus on what really matters—equipping children with practical financial skills that will serve them throughout their lives.

This book stands out because it's built around real-life applications and everyday relevance. We recognize the universal importance of financial literacy and respect the diverse cultural attitudes towards money and saving. By steering clear of fear-inducing and overly complex adult financial topics, we focus solely on what's appropriate and impactful for children.

You, the reader, are pivotal. Whether you're a parent, educator, or guardian, your role is crucial in shaping a child's perspective on money. This book is designed to support you in that role, offering a clear and effective roadmap to introduce essential financial lessons.

Structured to engage young minds, the book progresses from simple concepts like earning and saving to more dynamic topics such as smart spending and the basics of investing, all explained in kid-friendly terms. Plus, we've peppered the book with interactive sections, quizzes, and real-life challenges to ensure that the lessons stick.

Our customer research revealed a strong desire for a book that balances educational content with interactive learning. This feedback has been instrumental in shaping a book that meets your needs and exceeds your expectations.

So, as you turn these pages, I invite you to dive in actively. Engage with each chapter not just as a source of information but as an essential step in preparing your child for a financially sound future. Together, let's begin this journey, ensuring our kids are not just informed but also excited about the world of money.

And remember, it's never too early to start. The seeds of financial wisdom you plant today will grow into the smart money decisions of tomorrow. Let's make learning about money a rewarding adventure for our children, setting them on the path to a lifetime of financial confidence and success.

Chapter 1: Understanding Money Basics

———

Have you ever plopped down on the couch with a bowl of popcorn to watch a movie and found yourself diving into the cushions in search of some spare change? Maybe you were hunting for just enough to tip the pizza delivery guy, or perhaps to feed your growling piggy bank. Whatever the case, it's clear: money, in some way or another, is often a part of our daily adventures. But what's the real story behind those coins and crumpled bills, or even those numbers that magically appear in your banking app? Well, buckle up! We're about to take a lighthearted leap into the world of money, exploring not only what it is but also why we squirrel it away or sometimes spend it like it's burning a hole in our pockets.

<u>What is Money Really? Exploring the Idea of Exchange</u>

Definition and History

So, what is money? At its core, money is a medium of exchange. This means it's something widely accepted in exchange for goods and services. Imagine trying to buy your favorite video game by trading three chickens and a sack of potatoes. Sounds messy, right? That's where money comes in as a handy alternative to bartering with livestock or veggies. Historically, various items have been used as money. From shells and salt to precious metals like gold and silver, what qualified as money simply depended on what everyone agreed was valuable and practical.

Forms of Money

Fast forward to today, and money has had quite the makeover! We've moved from trading tangible items like those shiny metals to using coins and paper money, and now, digital forms are all the rage. Each form of money reflects the needs and technologies of the time. Coins made from metals were durable and portable, unlike livestock or grains. Paper money, introduced as a promise to pay the bearer a certain amount of precious metal, was lighter and easier to carry in larger amounts. Today, digital money moves invisibly and instantaneously around the globe, perfectly suited for our fast-paced, interconnected world.

Functions of Money

Money plays a crucial trio of roles: it's our go-to for trading, a way to keep score of what things cost, and our financial safety net. Imagine money as a superhero of trade, swooping in to make exchanging goods a breeze simply because everyone agrees on its worth. It's also like a scoreboard, helping us figure out how much things cost so we can manage our spending, whether we're saving up for cool kicks or a new game. Lastly, think of money as a piggy bank for the future, holding on to its value and waiting for you to break it open for something awesome. Saving for that rad skateboard or must-have tech gadget? It's the trust that your stash of cash will hold its value over time, ensuring you can snag your prize when you're all set.

Value of Money

Speaking of value, ever wondered why a piece of paper with a number on it can buy you something as valuable as a meal or a movie ticket? It all boils down to trust and a system backed by governments. When you accept money in exchange for something, you trust that this money will be accepted by others in turn. This trust is crucial and is backed by national governments which regulate and uphold the value of money through various complex mechanisms. This system works remarkably well, ensuring that, at least in most scenarios, money keeps its value and remains exchangeable for goods and services.

Grasping these ideas might initially feel as challenging as navigating a maze in the dark, but as you begin to understand how they fit into your everyday activities, it all becomes much clearer. Reflect on when you diligently saved your allowance for that must-have item. It was your understanding of how money works that made it possible, wasn't it? With this foundation, let's continue our adventure into the dynamic world of money, exploring its impact and movement in our lives with excitement and curiosity.

<u>The Journey of a Dollar: How Money Moves in the Economy</u>

Imagine a dollar bill snug in your wallet—it might feel like it's taking a little nap. But when it wakes up? Oh, the places it'll go! Money, you see, is quite the social butterfly in our economy, fluttering from hand to hand, fluttering into registers, and even zipping through wires in its digital form. Let's tag along on a day in the life of this dollar to see just how it makes the world go round, shall we?

Earning Money

First off, how does a dollar even find its way into your wallet? Well, it starts with earning. Picture this: Every week, you help around the house—maybe you're a vacuuming virtuoso or a dusting dynamo. When the chores are done, your parents hand you a few dollars. That's you, earning money! It's not just chores, though. People earn money in all sorts of ways, from designing buildings as architects to baking pastries as chefs. What all these jobs have in common is that they provide services or create things that others value. Money typically enters circulation when people or companies pay for these goods and services. It's the economy's way of saying, "Hey, thanks for that neat thing you did!"

Spending Money

Now, let's follow our dollar on its next adventure—spending! Say you've been eyeing a new comic book. You take your hard-earned dollar to the store, hand it over, and—voila!—that comic book is yours. But the journey doesn't stop there. The store might use your dollar to pay their employees, buy more comic books, or even pay for their electricity. Each time the dollar changes hands, it's helping people buy what they need or want. Businesses keep the economy buzzing by using the money from sales to cover their costs and to pay their own bills. This cycle of spending keeps shops open, workers paid, and, yes, keeps comic books stocked on the shelves.

Saving and Investing

Sometimes a dollar doesn't get spent right away. Instead, it goes into savings. Think of saving like giving your money a little vacation. You tuck it away in a bank, and while it relaxes there, it can grow. Banks use your saved dollars to make loans to other people who might need some cash to fix up their house or pay for college. These loans make money for the bank by charging a bit of interest, and some of that money comes back to you as more dollars. Investing works a bit like saving but can be a bit riskier, like lending money to companies by buying their stock. If the company does well, your money grows! If not, well, it's like lending a comic book to a friend who moves away—you might not see it again. But whether saving or investing, these activities help pump money through the economy, supporting everything from home-building to education.

Government's Role

And we can't forget about the government's role in all of this. The government is like the referee in the game of money, setting the rules that help keep everything fair. They print money—yes, they decide when to make more bills and coins. But their job doesn't stop there. They also use money to pay for things we all rely on, like schools and roads. They collect taxes from people and businesses, which might seem like a bummer, but those taxes help pay for the playgrounds you play in and the libraries where you find your favorite books. Plus, the government steps in to regulate banks and make sure they're treating your savings fairly.

So, there you have it—the life and times of a dollar in our bustling economy. From earning to spending, saving, and even paying taxes, every dollar you touch is on a vibrant tour of the economic world. Next time you spend a dollar, think about all the hands it will pass through and all the lives it will touch. It's not just money; it's a little ambassador of your values and choices, zipping around the economy and making a difference in countless ways.

Earning Your First Money: Ways Kids Can Earn at Home

Allowances for Chores

Chores might not always be fun, but they're a great way for kids to earn their first bit of money. Think of it as transforming everyday tasks into exciting challenges. Kids become secret agents on missions like "Operation Clean the Kitchen" or "The Great Laundry Fold." Completing these missions doesn't just earn them some cash; it turns mundane tasks into thrilling quests. This approach teaches kids the importance of hard work and responsibility. Every chore they finish is like a mini-job, contributing to the household and boosting their savings. It's an age-appropriate introduction to the concept of earning money, emphasizing that it's something earned rather than given, making the value of their earnings more meaningful.

Creative Projects

For those with a flair for entrepreneurship, embarking on a venture like a lemonade stand or a crafting project can be both enjoyable and financially beneficial. Imagine setting up a lemonade stand on a sunny day, serving refreshments to your neighbors while earning some extra pocket money. Or, during festive seasons, creating and selling handmade greeting cards or decorations could become quite popular. These ventures are more than just earning opportunities—they serve as hands-on lessons in economics, covering fundamentals such as supply and demand, costs, profits, and marketing strategies. It's about recognizing what others might need or enjoy and figuring out how to offer that with a unique twist. Plus, the pride in earning money through one's creativity is immensely satisfying. It's about putting passion into practice and seeing tangible rewards from those efforts.

Gifts and Rewards

Gifts and Rewards: A Learning Opportunity Special days like birthdays and holidays often bring the excitement of receiving cash or checks as gifts. Though this money isn't earned through chores or projects, it presents an excellent chance to learn about managing unexpected money gains. It's not merely about the immediate happiness that comes with receiving money; rather, it's an opportunity to make thoughtful decisions on how to utilize it effectively. Teaching kids to perhaps save a portion, spend a little, and maybe even share some with others provides a balanced approach to handling financial gifts. Moreover, rewards for achievements, whether academic or otherwise, can reinforce the value of striving for excellence. It's a way of showing that hard work and dedication can have tangible benefits beyond just the satisfaction of achieving goals.

Educational Incentives

Switching gears, let's dive into a topic that's often flying under the radar: educational incentives. Schools and various educational programs occasionally spotlight top achievers with rewards like scholarships, bonds, or even cash prizes. Engaging in competitions, whether it's showcasing a science project, solving complex math problems at an Olympiad, or devouring books for a reading challenge, might lead to financial rewards alongside recognition. However, the true treasure isn't the monetary reward—it's the rich experience and knowledge these adventures bestow. The monetary aspect merely adds a sprinkle of excitement to the quest for knowledge, making the pursuit of academic excellence even more appealing. These avenues offer more than mere opportunities to pocket some extra money; they're crucial building blocks for grasping the broader aspects of the economic world. They serve as foundational lessons in not only finance but also inculcate values of responsibility, spark creativity, and underscore the importance of education. They illustrate that money is not merely for spending but can be cultivated through one's endeavors and choices. So, when contemplating how to introduce your child to the concept of earning, remember that it transcends just acquiring cash. It's about nurturing the skills and values that will enrich them far beyond their initial earnings.

<u>The Power of Saving: Why We Save and How It Grows</u>

Saving money might not sound as thrilling as spending it—after all, who doesn't get a little rush from buying the latest gadget or snagging that cool pair of sneakers? But here's a little secret: saving can be just as exciting. Think of it as a treasure hunt where every coin you stash away brings you closer to unearthing that big prize you've been eyeing. Whether it's a new bike, a family vacation, or that high-tech drone, saving is your ticket to turning those dreams into reality. And while we're digging into this, let's explore why building this treasure chest is crucial not just for those big wishes, but for your overall financial security.

Reasons to Save

So, why do we save? For starters, life is full of surprises. Some are great—like an unexpected gift or a surprise party. But others, like a sudden need for car repairs or a last-minute school project, might have you scrambling for spare cash. Having money set aside in savings means these hiccups don't have to knock the wind out of your sails. It's like having a financial safety net that catches you, letting you deal with unexpected expenses without stress. Saving is also about planning for bigger goals. Want to upgrade your gaming console or set out on a grand family adventure? A well-fed savings account means these goals don't just stay wishes—they become achievable plans. And let's not forget about the ultimate goal: future security. Saving consistently helps ensure that down the road, you're set up for things like college or even your first car.

Interest Explained

Now, let's jazz things up a bit and talk about how your money can actually grow while it's sitting in savings. This little magic trick is called 'interest'. Simply put, when you save your money in a bank, the bank pays you a small amount for letting them hold onto it. It's like if you let a friend borrow a video game, and when they returned it, they gave you a bonus game as a thank you. Except in this case, the bonus comes in the form of extra money! Banks use your money to give out loans to others, and the interest they charge on these loans allows them to pay you that little extra. Over time, this interest adds up, helping your savings grow without you having to do a thing. It's your money's way of saying, 'Thanks for saving me!'

Goals for Saving

Setting savings goals makes the whole process a lot more fun and concrete. Let's say, for example, you're dreaming of owning a new skateboard. First, find out how much it costs. Let's peg it at $100 for simplicity. Now, decide when you'd like to buy it—maybe three months from now. That means you need to save about $33 each month. Break it down further: that's just over a dollar a day! Suddenly, your goal feels a lot more achievable, right? Whether it's saving for a new toy, a book, or even a cool field trip, having clear goals helps you stay focused and makes saving feel like a game where every little bit saved is a step closer to victory.

Tools for Saving

The beauty of saving today is that there's a whole arsenal of tools at your disposal, designed to make the process both fun and fruitful. Let's start with the quintessential piggy bank—a timeless favorite for the younger crowd. It's more than just an adorable decor item; it's a visual and tactile motivator for kids to watch their savings grow, coin by coin. Moving into the digital age, there's a plethora of apps tailored for the young and tech-savvy. These applications aren't just about stashing cash away; they transform saving into an interactive adventure. Kids can set saving targets, monitor their progress, and engage with educational content that makes learning about money management exciting. And of course, we can't forget about the traditional savings account. Tailored specifically for young savers, many banks offer these accounts with minimal fees and low entry requirements. They're not just a safe haven for funds; they're a learning tool, offering features like online banking that allow savers to observe their money's growth in real-time. These resources do more than aid in saving—they're building blocks for a lifetime of financial wisdom. Whether you're dropping change into a piggy bank, navigating savings goals on an app, or making a deposit into a savings account, each action is a step toward a future where you're in control, equipped with the confidence and know-how that come from mastering the art of saving.

Basic Budgeting: Planning Your Spending and Saving

Picture this: you're at a candy store, eyes wide at the kaleidoscope of sweets—a veritable treasure trove of sugary delights. You've got five bucks, a heart full of desire, and a head swirling with choices. Here's where the magic of budgeting comes into play, transforming you from a wide-eyed candy spender to a savvy sweet shopper. A budget, simply put, is your plan for navigating the candy store of life. It's about knowing how much money you have, deciding what you need to spend it on, and figuring out what you want to save for—be it a mountain of marshmallows or something a bit more substantial down the line.

So, how do you create this magical financial plan? Start with what you've got—this could be your allowance, money from chores, or that birthday cash from Grandma. Let's say you've got $20 this month. Now, think about your expenses. These could be things like a new notebook for school or saving for that video game you've been eyeing, which costs $60. By deciding to save, say, $5 each month, you'll be gaming in a year's time without breaking a sweat. This basic formula of income minus expenses equals savings is your golden ticket to budgeting success.

But life, as you know, loves throwing curveballs. Maybe this month, you have a school trip that costs $10, which you hadn't planned for in your budget. No panic needed—this is where adjusting your budget comes in handy. Maybe you cut back on some treats or postpone buying that notebook. Adjusting your budget means staying flexible and ready to shuffle your funds around to cover both your needs and wants without derailing your financial goals. It's like being the captain of your own ship, steering through the sea of expenses and savings, making sure you navigate smoothly to reach your financial goals without getting lost.

Now, for the fun part—let's try some practical budgeting activities. How about planning a family movie night? Here's the challenge: you have $30 to make a night to remember. You'd need to budget for snacks, maybe a rented movie, or even some cozy blankets. Decide what's essential and what's not. Maybe popcorn is a must, but store-bought soda can be swapped for some homemade lemonade. This activity not only makes budgeting real but shows how decisions can stretch your dollar further to include more of what you love.

Another engaging way to practice is through virtual budgeting games. Many online platforms offer simulations where you're given a virtual income and a list of potential expenses and savings goals. You get to decide how to allocate your virtual funds to achieve different objectives, all while navigating the unexpected expenses that the game throws your way. It's like playing the role of a financial superhero, where saving the day means balancing that budget to perfection.

By diving into these activities, the concept of budgeting transforms from just crunching numbers to becoming an essential, lively tool that gives you the power to shape your financial journey, one wise decision at a time. Whether you're squirreling away funds for a grand goal or simply seeking the best value during your next visit to the candy shop, becoming proficient in budgeting is a priceless ability that will guide you through the many quests life has in store. So, when you next hold money in your grasp, bear in mind: a budget is more than a mere blueprint. It's your passport to making the most of your money, ensuring that every dollar you spend or save is a step toward achieving your dreams.

<u>Needs vs. Wants: Learning to Prioritize at a Young Age</u>

When it comes to teaching kids about money, one of the most valuable lessons revolves around understanding the difference between needs and wants. Picture this: you're in the toy aisle with your child, and their eyes light up at the sight of the latest superhero action figure. "I need this," they declare with the seriousness of a seasoned negotiator. This is the perfect moment for a practical, on-the-spot money lesson. Needs are essentials, the must-haves for daily living, like food, shelter, and clothing. Wants, on the other hand, are all the extras. They're the cherry on top—nice to have but not necessary for survival or basic comfort.

This distinction might seem straightforward to us as adults, but for kids, it can be a bit blurry. Everything can feel like a 'need' when you really, really want it, right? That's why it's crucial to discuss this with children, helping them understand that while it's okay to want things, prioritizing needs is essential. This lesson isn't just about budgeting; it's about values and making choices that align with them. When children learn to identify and prioritize their needs over their wants, they're not just learning how to manage money; they're learning how to manage life.

Now, let's talk about how we can foster these decision-making skills in our young ones. It starts with open conversations. The next time your child receives money, whether it's from chores or a birthday, sit down and chat about what they plan to do with it. If they're eyeing something that falls squarely in the 'wants' category, that's okay. Use this as an opportunity to discuss the importance of also saving for needs or future important expenses. You can introduce the idea of waiting periods—a powerful way to curb impulse buys. Suggest waiting a day or two before purchasing that sought-after toy. Often, after a night's sleep, the 'need' for the latest gadget or gizmo diminishes, and sometimes, they might decide to save or spend on something more meaningful.

Why not transform these key concepts into an engaging game? This interactive, scenario-based learning method brings financial decisions to life. Imagine setting up a game where your child, equipped with a set amount of pretend money, must make a series of spending choices. Transform your living room into a financial decision-making playground, with areas marked for 'needs'—such as essential groceries, school necessities, or a savings pot for future education—and 'wants,' which could include luxury items like video games, toys, or theme park visits. As they navigate through these stations, deciding where to allocate their funds, it presents the perfect opportunity for discussion.

This tactile approach not only aids in grasping the significance of their choices but also highlights the joy of spending wisely.

Engaging children in these kinds of activities not only makes learning about money fun but also embeds deep-seated financial wisdom that they will carry into adulthood. As they grow, this understanding of needs versus wants will guide their spending habits, influence their saving behaviors, and shape their overall approach to money. And perhaps, during your next trip to the toy store, you'll hear something like, "I want this, but I don't really need it right now," and you'll know that the seeds of financial prudence are starting to sprout. This approach doesn't just prepare them for the financial challenges of adulthood—it equips them to face them with confidence and a clear understanding of what truly matters in their financial and personal lives.

Chapter 2: Smart Money Management

———

Ever found yourself on a seesaw, teetering between splurging on that jumbo ice cream sundae and saving for that cool, new bike? That's a bit what managing money feels like, doesn't it? Well, don't sweat it! We're about to embark on a delightful romp through the world of smart money management, where learning to balance your financial seesaw will turn you from a spender to a saver, and dare I say, a financial wizard in the making!

In this chapter, let's kick things off by setting up a savings plan that even the most enthusiastic spender will find manageable and yes, even fun! We'll explore how to set goals that get you pumped, design a roadmap to reach those dreams, utilize tools that make saving a breeze, and keep track of your progress like a pro. So, grab your financial cape (yes, you have one!), and let's make some savings magic happen!

<u>Setting Up a Savings Plan: Tips for Young Savers</u>

Establishing Savings Goals

Imagine you're a captain setting sail on the high seas; your savings goal is your treasure map, guiding you to the loot—be it a new skateboard, the latest video game, or making a generous donation to your favorite charity. The trick is to pick destinations (goals) that really spark excitement and are important to you. This isn't just about stashing cash away for a rainy day; it's about saving with a purpose, which makes the journey a whole lot more thrilling. Sit down with your young ones and chat about what they're passionate about. Is it art? Maybe saving for some premium art supplies could be the goal. Sports? Perhaps a new set of team jerseys or equipment. Whatever it is, make sure these goals are clear, achievable, and most importantly, meaningful to them. This turns saving from a mundane task into a personal mission, something they can look forward to achieving.

Creating a Savings Timeline

Now that we have our treasure map, we need to chart the course. This is where a savings timeline comes into play. It's all about breaking down that big, scary goal into smaller, manageable islands of achievement. If a video game console is the goal and it costs $300, figure out how much time we want to give ourselves to reach it. Six months, maybe? That breaks down to saving $50 a month. But let's make it even simpler—about $12.50 a week. Suddenly, that mountain of a goal seems like a series of small, easy hills to climb! Setting up a timeline not only keeps us on track but also divides our goal into bite-sized pieces that are much easier to digest and achieve. It's like turning a daunting diet into a series of simple, healthy meals.

Using Savings Tools

In our treasure chest of savings tools, there's something for every type of saver. For the traditionalists, a good old piggy bank never goes out of style. But let's crank it up a notch. There are now digital piggy banks that not only store coins but also track how much has been saved, adding a bit of tech flair to the classic saving method. Then there are savings accounts specifically designed for kids, often with no fees and fun incentives to save more. These accounts are great because they introduce kids to the banking system in a friendly, approachable way, and they often come with mobile apps that allow kids (and parents) to check in on their progress anytime, anywhere. It's like having a financial dashboard for your savings journey—how cool is that?

Monitoring and Adjusting Plans

Even the best-laid plans may need some tweaking, and that's perfectly okay. Think of it as being the director of your own movie. Sometimes, a scene doesn't work out the way you thought it would, and you need to adjust the script. The same goes for your savings plan. Regular check-ins on your savings progress are crucial. They help you see if you're on track or if you need to tweak your tactics. Maybe you find extra chores to do around the house to boost your savings, or perhaps you decide to extend your timeline a bit to make the saving less stressful. The key is to stay flexible and proactive, making adjustments as needed to keep the savings voyage smooth sailing. This approach not only keeps you adaptable but also teaches a valuable life lesson: it's okay to revise your plans to better suit your circumstances.

Navigating through these aspects of setting up a savings plan might initially seem like trying to solve a puzzle in the dark. But with each goal set, each timeline drawn, and each tool used, the pieces start to fit together, lighting up the path to financial savvy. And remember, this isn't just about reaching one goal; it's about building the skills and habits that will empower you, the fantastic financial mentor, to guide your young savers towards a future where they not only reach but also create new and exciting financial destinations on their own. So, cheers to making saving a part of your family's adventure—a journey that promises not just financial rewards, but also invaluable life lessons woven through the fun and challenges of smart money management.

<u>Fun With Budgets: Interactive Budgeting Activities</u>

Imagine transforming the sometimes snooze-worthy subject of budgeting into a thrilling board game night or a lively role-play session where you and the kids get to be the stars of your own financial drama series. That's right! We're about to dive into the world of budgeting through play, making it as delightful as scooping up the last piece of your favorite pie. Who said learning about money management had to be a chore? Grab your props, your colorful pens, and maybe even your calculator—it's time to make budgeting a blast!

Let's kick things off with budgeting games. Think of this as your personal financial playground. How about a game where each child runs a small business? Picture a lemonade stand, but with a twist. Each kid gets a set amount of imaginary money to "invest" in their stand. They'll need to think about costs like lemons, sugar, and cups, and then decide how much to sell their lemonade for. As the game progresses, they'll see how their decisions affect their business's success. Or, let's set the scene for a holiday planning session. Here, kids are given a budget and a list of potential holiday expenses like travel, food, and entertainment. Their goal? To plan a holiday that's fun yet stays within budget. These games teach valuable lessons about cost management, profit calculation, and strategic planning, all while keeping the fun meter cranked up to high.

Now, who's ready for some budget role-playing? This is where things get really interactive. Set up a mock household and assign roles: perhaps one child is the breadwinner, another is in charge of grocery shopping, and another manages utilities and leisure. Give them a monthly "income" and a list of expenses they must manage. As they navigate through paying bills, saving for emergencies, and maybe squeezing in a movie night or a family outing, they'll learn the intricate dance of income versus outgoings. This role-play isn't just about numbers; it's about making choices and dealing with the consequences of those choices, providing a safe space to explore financial decision-making.

Crafting budget boards is another visually engaging way to bring budgeting to life. This activity can be as simple as grabbing a large piece of poster board and dividing it into sections for income, savings, and expenses. Have kids decorate their boards with stickers, drawings, or photos that represent their financial goals. They can use markers to track their progress, adding a tactile and visual element to their budgeting practice. This not just aids in keeping track of finances but also serves as a daily reminder of their goals and progress, making the abstract concept of budget management concrete and understandable.

Lastly, let's tap into the digital age with some child-friendly budgeting apps or software. These tools are designed to make budgeting appealing and accessible. Many apps feature engaging interfaces, fun characters, and interactive challenges that teach kids about budgeting, saving, and spending wisely. They can see their financial scenarios play out in real time, adjust their budgets with a swipe, and get instant feedback on their financial decisions. It's like having a mini financial advisor right at their fingertips, one that speaks their language and grows with them as they learn more about managing money effectively.

Through these interactive budgeting activities, we're not merely teaching kids the nuts and bolts of money management—we're instilling life skills. Integrating playful elements into financial education dismantles the daunting barriers often associated with money matters, transforming it into an enjoyable, enlightening journey. Kids are doing more than just playing; through negotiation, strategy, and celebrating their achievements in these activities, they're laying the groundwork for real-world financial savvy, all while wearing big smiles.

<u>Wise Spending: Making Smart Choices</u>

Let's be honest, navigating the maze of money decisions can sometimes feel like trying to choose the best doughnut at a bustling bakery—everything looks good, but not all choices are equal. Wise spending isn't just about clamping down on your wallet; it's about making choices that give you the biggest bang for your buck, and teaching this to kids can turn them into savvy spenders before they even hit their teens.

Let's unwrap this concept of 'value for money' together, shall we? Imagine you're eyeing a shiny new scooter. One costs more but comes with extra features like better brakes and a warranty, while the cheaper one, well, it's pretty basic. Here's where you play detective—weighing the benefits against the cost. If that scooter will be your daily ride for years, investing a bit more upfront for extra safety and durability makes sense. This approach isn't just about spending less; it's about spending smart and getting the most out of every dollar.

Now, onto the battlefield of needs vs. wants—a classic financial tug-of-war. Here's how you can make it a teaching moment. Picture this: your kid has money from a birthday and is itching to spend it all on a new video game. This is the perfect time to chat about prioritizing spending on needs before wants. Maybe they need new shoes for school or have been saving for a special class trip. Discussing how to use their funds to cover these needs first teaches them to plan their spending, laying a foundation for managing bigger budgets down the line. Any leftover money can then be a gateway to discussing saving or occasionally treating themselves. It's about creating a balance that lets them enjoy their money while also meeting their needs.

Peer pressure—it's like the sneaky villain in our spending story, always lurking around the corner, especially for kids. It's tough seeing friends with the latest gadgets or fashion and feeling left out. Here's where you step in with some superhero guidance. Teach them about making independent, well-considered financial choices. It's okay to say no to trends and yes to what really matters to them or fits their budget. Role-playing can be a great way to practice these scenarios. Set up a situation where they have to choose between going with the crowd or sticking to their financial plan. This not only prepares them for real-life situations but also boosts their confidence in making decisions that are right for them, not just what's popular.

Finally, let's make spending wisely a celebratory affair! Setting up a rewards system for making smart spending decisions can turn what might seem like a chore into a challenge with perks. For instance, if they decide to save money by buying a more cost-effective item or skip an unnecessary purchase, reward them with something like extra playtime, a favorite meal, or even the responsibility of choosing the next family activity. These rewards reinforce the positive behavior, making the learning process enjoyable and memorable. It's a way of saying, 'Hey, great job on that smart money move! Here's a little something to show you that being financially savvy doesn't just pay off in the long run—it's also fun right now.'

Navigating spending decisions with kids in this way isn't just about teaching them to count pennies; it's about helping them understand the value of money and empowering them to make choices that align with their goals and needs. By discussing value for money, prioritizing needs, managing peer pressure, and celebrating wise spending, you're equipping them with skills for a lifetime of smart financial decisions. So next time you hit the stores or browse online, remember, each spending decision is more than a transaction—it's an opportunity to teach and learn, and maybe, just maybe, make saving as exciting as spending.

<u>The Art of Comparison Shopping</u>

Imagine you're on a treasure hunt, not in some far-off jungle, but right in the bustling aisles of your local shopping center or the endless digital shelves of online stores. Your quest? To snag the best deals on your most wanted items—be it a cool new skateboard, the latest best-selling children's book, or that trendy backpack everyone at school is talking about. This adventure is called comparison shopping, and it's not just a way to save a few bucks—it's a strategy to maximize your spending power and sharpen your financial savvy.

Let's dive into how to compare prices effectively. Picture this: you're eyeing a popular video game priced at $50 in a store. Hold up—don't grab it just yet! A quick search online might show that it's available for $45 at another retailer, and maybe there's a special promo code that knocks an additional $5 off. Just like that, you've saved $10 with a few taps on your smartphone or clicks of your mouse. This is comparison shopping in action. It involves checking various stores and online platforms to find where your desired item is being sold at the lowest price. It's like being a detective, where every clue (or in this case, every dollar saved) leads you closer to solving the case of the elusive best deal.

Now, onto the dazzling world of sales and discounts. Sales can seem like the ultimate way to save money, but they come with their own set of traps. Here's the lowdown: not all sales are as good as they seem. Sometimes, stores mark up prices right before a big sale, so the 'discounted' price may not be much lower than the usual selling price. This is where your sharp detective skills come in again. Track the prices of items over time, or use price-tracking tools available on many websites to see the price history. This way, you can tell if that discount is a real steal or just a clever marketing trick. And when deciphering discounts, always calculate the final price after the discount to ensure it's within your budget and worth your dollars.

Let's talk about quality versus price. It's tempting to go for cheaper options to save money, but this isn't always the best move in the long run. Think about it like this: buying a pair of shoes that are a bit more expensive but are well-made and durable is better than opting for a cheaper pair that falls apart after a few wears. Initially, it feels like you're spending more, but if the pricier item lasts longer, you won't need to replace it as soon, which means more savings over time. It's all about looking at purchases as investments rather than just one-time buys. So, when you're comparing prices, also consider the longevity and quality of the items. Sometimes, spending a bit more upfront can actually be a more economical choice in the grand scheme of things.

Lastly, let's unlock the potential of coupons and cashback offers, the superheroes of savvy shopping. Coupons can slash your checkout price, while cashback rewards you with a percentage of your purchase back in cash. It sounds pretty sweet, right? Here's how to make the most of these deals: keep an eye out for coupons in store newsletters, on coupon websites, and in local newspapers. For online shopping, browser extensions can automatically find and apply the best coupons for your purchases. As for cashback, several credit cards and shopping apps offer this perk, so do your research and use them wisely. Just remember, the key to maximizing these benefits is to use coupons and cashback for things you were already planning to buy, not as an excuse to spend more.

In this whirlwind tour of comparison shopping, you're not just learning to spot the best prices or to dissect sales and discounts; you're mastering the art of making every dollar work harder for you. This isn't just about being thrifty; it's about being smart and strategic with your spending, ensuring you get the best value while still nabbing all the things you love and need. So, the next time you set out on your shopping expedition, remember these tips and tricks. With a keen eye for deals, a smart approach to quality, and the magic of coupons and cashback, you're all set to become a champion comparison shopper, turning every shopping trip into a financially savvy adventure.

<u>Avoiding Impulse Buying: Strategies for Thoughtful Purchases</u>

You know the drill—you walk into a store or browse online, and something shiny catches your eye. Suddenly, you're reaching for your wallet, convinced that you absolutely need this new gadget, toy, or treat, right now. But let's hit the pause button on that shopping spree and talk about a really neat trick: the 'waiting period' rule. It's like putting a time-out on your spending habits, giving you and your kids a chance to think over a purchase before diving in. Here's how it works: whenever you or your kids feel the urge to buy something on the spot, decide to wait a day or two before making the purchase. Use this time to discuss and reflect on whether this item is a need, a genuine want, or just a spur-of-the-moment desire. This little pause can be incredibly powerful. It turns an impulsive decision into a thoughtful choice, giving you time to evaluate the importance and necessity of the item. Maybe after a day, that 'must-have' item doesn't seem so crucial anymore. Or perhaps, you find a better price elsewhere (a victory for our comparison shopping skills!). By implementing this rule, you're teaching your kids an invaluable lesson in self-control and decision-making, skills that will benefit them way beyond the checkout line.

Now, let's chat about the magic of maintaining a wishlist. This isn't just any list—it's a dynamic tool that helps manage both desires and finances. Encourage your kids to jot down things they want on this wishlist and then prioritize these items based on their interests and the value these items bring. Periodically review this list together, maybe once a month or with each change of season. This review session is a great opportunity to discuss why certain items are on the list and if they should stay there. Is that video game from six months ago still a favorite, or has it lost its charm? This practice not only keeps impulsive buying in check but also helps refine and understand what truly brings joy and value to their lives. Plus, it's a fun way to plan potential rewards for special occasions or achievements!

Emotional spending—now that's a tricky beast. It could be the ice cream after a bad day or splurging on a new toy to celebrate good grades. While treating ourselves can feel good, it's crucial to recognize these emotional triggers for what they are. Start conversations around how emotions can influence spending decisions. Discuss times when feelings might have led to unnecessary purchases and explore healthier ways to handle those emotions, like talking about a tough day or celebrating with a fun, cost-free activity. By making kids aware of these triggers, you empower them to handle their emotions without opening their wallets. It's about finding joy and comfort in experiences rather than just material goods, a lesson that even us adults could benefit from revisiting now and then.

Lastly, let's set the stage for setting spending limits. This is like drawing a treasure map where X marks how much can be spent on different categories like toys, snacks, or outings. Sit down with your kids and decide together on reasonable limits for these categories. This could be a weekly or monthly budget, depending on their age and understanding. Having clear boundaries helps kids make more informed choices about their spending and teaches them to balance their budget—a crucial skill for their future financial health. Whether it's deciding how much to spend on a weekend outing or how many treats they can pick at the grocery store, these limits help instill a sense of financial discipline and planning. Plus, it turns everyday decisions into mini-budgeting lessons, making the concept of money management a natural part of their daily life.

Through these strategies, you're not just curbing impulse buys; you're setting the foundation for thoughtful, informed purchasing decisions. It's about creating a mindful approach to spending, where every dollar spent is considered and valued. This doesn't just help keep your bank account happy; it builds a mindset that appreciates and maximizes the worth of money, ensuring that when your kids do decide to make a purchase, it's truly something meaningful and well-considered. So, next time that impulse to buy strikes, remember, a little pause, a well-maintained wishlist, an understanding of emotional spending, and clear spending limits can transform a potential splurge into a power move in personal finance.

<u>Saving for a Big Goal: Steps to Success</u>

When it comes to teaching kids about saving for big goals—whether it's a new bike, a family vacation, or that fancy treehouse they've been dreaming about—it can often feel a bit like explaining why they need to eat their veggies: good for them, but not always easy to swallow. The trick is to make the process as fun and digestible as possible. Let's break down those big dreams into smaller, achievable steps that even the most impatient saver can manage.

First up, let's tackle the art of breaking down large goals. Imagine your child wants a new gaming console. The price tag makes you wince—it's steep! But instead of seeing this as one gigantic mountain of cash, break it down together into smaller molehills. If the console costs $300, and your child can save $50 a month, in just six months, they'll be ready to play their favorite games on their new console. By dividing the total into smaller, more manageable parts, the goal suddenly seems a lot less daunting. This practice not only makes the goal seem achievable but also teaches valuable lessons about planning and patience.

Next, we dive into the world of incremental saving strategies. It's all about taking baby steps. Encourage your kids to set aside a small amount of money regularly—be it from their weekly allowance, birthday cash, or money earned from small jobs like pet-sitting or lemonade stands. Even a few dollars saved every week can add up surprisingly fast. It's like building a Lego set; each small piece contributes to creating something awesome. Help them find creative ways to boost their savings. Maybe they decide to skip buying a snack at school once a week or opt for a more affordable outing with friends, redirecting those savings towards their bigger goal.

Now, let's add some color and fun with visual progress tracking. There's nothing quite as motivating as seeing your efforts pay off, and for kids, visual cues are particularly impactful. Use charts, apps, or even a simple jar where they can drop in coins and watch their savings grow. You could create a colorful chart that tracks progress with stickers or markers, or use a digital app that visualizes savings in fun, engaging ways. Every time they add to their savings, they get to fill in a bit more of their chart or see their virtual savings jar fill up on the screen. This not only makes saving more tangible but also injects a sense of fun into the process.

Celebrating milestones is crucial. Just like adults need to see progress in their endeavors, kids also need to feel like their hard work is paying off. Set mini-goals along the way to the big one, and find small, meaningful ways to celebrate when they reach them. Maybe after saving the first $50, they get to pick out a small toy, or you can have a family movie night. These celebrations help maintain motivation and focus, making the saving journey enjoyable rather than just a long grind towards a distant goal. It's about enjoying the ride, not just waiting for the destination.

Through these steps, saving for a big goal transforms from an overwhelming challenge into an exciting adventure, broken down into enjoyable, manageable stages. It teaches kids about the value of money, yes, but also about patience, perseverance, and the satisfaction of working towards something important. And as they grow, these lessons build a foundation for financial confidence and competence that extends well beyond childhood savings.

In wrapping up this chapter, remember that teaching kids to save for big goals is about more than just numbers; it's about setting them up for future success. By breaking down large goals, using incremental saving strategies, tracking their progress visually, and celebrating milestones, you're helping them build a toolkit of skills and attitudes that will serve them throughout life. As we move forward, the focus shifts from saving to growing money, where the principles of investing will take center stage, showing kids the potential of their savings to not just sit but grow.

Chapter 3: Growing Your Money

———

Let's imagine you've just planted a tiny seed in your backyard. Each day, with a sprinkle of water and a bit of sunshine, that little seed starts to sprout into a flourishing plant. Now, isn't that a bit like putting your money into a savings account? Just as you nurture a seed to grow, you can nurture your savings to grow through the magic of interest. Think of interest as the sunshine for your savings—essential for growth. In this chapter, we'll dive into the basics of simple interest, transforming what might seem like dull numbers into a thrilling growth adventure for your money. We're not just saving here; we're growing, and that's where the real fun begins!

Understanding Interest

So, what exactly is interest? Let's break it down with a relatable example. Imagine you lend $10 to a friend so they can buy a snack, and they promise to pay you back $11 next week. That extra $1 is like a little "thank you" for lending them the money, and in the world of finance, we call it interest. When you save money in a bank, the bank uses your money to give out loans to others, just like you did with your friend. In return for using your money, the bank pays you interest. It's their way of saying "thanks" for letting them use your savings to help others.

This concept of earning money on your money is a powerful tool in the world of saving. It's like turning your saved money into a mini-worker whose job is to earn more money for you. The best part? You don't have to do anything extra—your money does the work while you sleep, go to school, or play. That's the beauty of interest!

Calculating Simple Interest

Now, how do we figure out how much interest you'll earn? It's time for a little math magic with a formula that's as easy as pie (and just as satisfying!): Interest = Principal x Rate x Time. Let's decode that, shall we?

Principal: This is just a fancy term for the amount of money you start with. If you put $100 in your savings account, that $100 is your principal.

Rate: This is the interest rate, which the bank will tell you when you open your account. It's usually a percentage. Let's say it's 5% per year in our example.

Time: This is how long you leave your money in the bank. Let's keep it simple and say it's 1 year for now.

<u>Plugging in the numbers</u>: Interest = $100 x 5% x 1 year = $5. That means, at the end of the year, you'll earn $5 in interest, just for keeping your $100 in the bank. Not too shabby for doing absolutely nothing, right?

Practical Examples

Let's bring this concept to life with a scenario you might find yourself in. Imagine you've been saving up for a new bike and you have $200 to start with. You decide to put this money in a savings account with a 3% interest rate. Using our trusty formula: Interest = $200 x 3% x 1 year = $6. So, by the end of the year, you'll have your initial $200 plus an extra $6, just from interest. It might seem small, but as you save more and keep it in the bank longer, these amounts add up, and your money continues to grow. It's like your initial savings have made little money friends over the year!

Encouraging Savings

Understanding how interest works can be a huge motivation to save more. It's thrilling to see your money grow, and the more you save, the more interest you earn, which then earns more interest on itself! It's a snowball effect that can significantly increase your savings over time. This is especially exciting when you're saving up for something big, like a video game console or a trip. Seeing the tangible results of your savings growing can inspire you to keep adding to your savings, nurturing it just like that little seed we talked about. Before you know, your small savings can grow into a mighty money tree.

In wrapping up this intro to simple interest, remember, the goal here isn't just to save money—it's to grow it. Interest is a powerful tool in your financial toolkit, helping turn your hard-earned money into even more money over time. By starting early, staying consistent, and using interest to your advantage, you're on your way to becoming not just a saver, but a smart saver. So, let's keep this growth journey going, watering our financial seeds with knowledge and watching them sprout into a flourishing future.

<u>Compound Interest Magic: How Your Money Multiplies</u>

Imagine your money is a tiny snowball at the top of a huge snowy hill. As it rolls down, it picks up more and more snow, growing bigger and faster with every turn. This snowball effect is a lot like compound interest in the world of saving and investing—it's how your money grows on itself over time, getting bigger and beefier without you needing to push it along! Let's unravel this magical concept and see how it transforms your finances, turning that initial snowball into a mighty avalanche of savings.

First up, let's clear the air about the difference between simple interest and compound interest. You already know that simple interest is like getting a thank you note in the form of money for lending out your cash. It's straightforward—you lend $100 at a 5% interest rate for a year, and you get $5 back. Simple, right? Well, compound interest is like that thank you note coming with a small gift that grows each time. With compound interest, not only do you earn interest on your initial amount (just like with simple interest), but you also earn interest on the interest that's been added to your account. It's interest on interest! Imagine if every time you helped out a friend, they not only thanked you but also offered a bigger and better thank to you the next time. Over time, those thanks would add up significantly.

Now, let's break down the formula for compound interest—it's not as intimidating as it sounds, I promise! The formula is: $A = P(1 + r/n)^{(nt)}$. Okay, let's decode that:

A is the amount of money you'll have after interest.

P is your principal, or initial amount.

r is the annual interest rate (decimal).

n is the number of times interest is compounded per year.

t is the number of years you save or invest your money.

Let's put that into a real-life scenario. Say you save $200 at an interest rate of 4% compounded annually for 5 years. Plugging those numbers into our formula gives us: $A = 200(1 + 0.04/1)^{(1*5)} = \$243.33$ approximately. So, after 5 years, your $200 turns into $243.33. You earned an extra $43.33 just by letting your money sit and grow!

Visualizing Compound Interest Growth

Getting a clear picture of how compound interest works can be a game-changer. Picture a graph: time is on the horizontal line, and money is on the vertical. You start with your first savings amount marked on the graph. With each passing year, as your interest earns more interest, your savings point shoots up higher and sharper. At first glance, the climb seems gradual, but as time flies, that upward trajectory gets steeper—showing how your savings initially grow bit by bit and then boom, they skyrocket. This isn't just a neat graph to look at; it's a powerful motivator. It transforms the concept of saving from a mere task into an exciting journey, urging you to keep on this path as your money blossoms into a significant stash.

Let's apply this concept to some real-life situations where compound interest is a game-changer. Consider a savings account you begin as a young saver. Each year, the interest earned is added to your original amount, and then the new total earns more interest. This process repeats year after year. Or think about investment bonds, where you invest a certain amount of money and it grows thanks to the magic of compounding, often at higher rates than a regular savings account. These scenarios aren't just hypothetical—they're real opportunities to see your money multiply through the power of compound interest.

Understanding and utilizing compound interest is like having a superpower in your financial toolkit. It encourages you to start saving early, because the sooner you start, the more your money can grow. It shows you that even small amounts, given enough time, can turn into impressive sums. Compound interest doesn't just add to your savings; it exponentially accelerates them, providing you with a greater sense of security and more possibilities for the future. So, why wait? Let your money start rolling down that snowy hill today, and watch as it builds into an avalanche of wealth, ready for you when you need it most.

<u>Simple Investments for Kids: Safe Ways to Grow Money</u>

When you think of investing, you might picture businessmen in suits, bustling stock exchanges, or maybe even those complicated financial charts that seem like they need a decoder ring just to understand. But guess what? Investing isn't just for grown-ups with briefcases; it's also for kids who want to see their money grow. Just like planting a seed that blossoms into a tree, investing is about putting your money into something that grows over time. Unlike keeping your money in a piggy bank or a savings account where it earns interest, investing can help your money grow faster and bigger, thanks to the magic of the market or other investment opportunities.

Let's start with a simple explanation. Investing is essentially putting your money into assets—like stocks, bonds, or real estate—with the expectation that your money will grow over time. Think of it as buying a tiny part of a company or lending your money to someone with the promise they'll pay you back with a bit more. Now, this isn't without risks, but the potential for higher returns can make it an exciting option beyond traditional saving.

One of the safest investment options for young investors is government bonds. Think of a bond as a kind of IOU where you lend money to the government, and in return, they promise to pay you back with interest after a certain period. It's like giving your friend a loan, knowing they're super reliable and will definitely pay you back. Government bonds are generally considered safe because they are backed by the government, so the risk of losing your money is low.

Another kid-friendly investment option is educational savings accounts, like the 529 Plan in the United States. These accounts allow parents to invest money that grows tax-free as long as you use it for educational purposes, like college tuition or textbooks. It's a smart way to save for education because it uses the power of investment growth to build up a fund over time, making it easier to manage those hefty education costs later on.

Now, let's chat about risk and return. Every investment has some level of risk, meaning there's a chance you might not get back as much money as you hoped, or you could even lose money. However, the potential for higher returns can make taking some risk worthwhile.

Safe investments like government bonds generally have lower returns because they have lower risk. It's like choosing a slow and steady turtle in a race; it might not be the fastest, but you know it'll reach the finish line. Teaching kids about this balance early on helps them make smarter, more informed decisions about where to put their money as they grow.

So, how can kids get started with investing? It's something you can do together. Start by having a conversation about goals and what they might want to save for—beyond the next cool video game. Maybe they want to save for college, or perhaps they'd like to buy a car when they turn sixteen. Once you have a goal in mind, you can look into opening a custodial account, which lets adults manage investments for minors. You can start small, maybe with buying a few government bonds or setting up a 529 Plan. As you watch these investments over time, discuss what's happening. Is the investment growing? What factors influence the growth? This can be a great way to learn together and for kids to get a hands-on education in how investing works.

Investing might sound complex, but it's just another way to make your money work for you, and it's not just for adults. By starting early, kids can learn the ropes of investing with you as their guide, turning those initial small investments into a growing fund that can help them achieve their dreams. Whether it's buying bonds, exploring educational savings accounts, or even eventually dabbling in stocks, the world of investing is a fertile field that, when navigated wisely, can yield plentiful returns for the future.

The Rule of 72 for Kids: Doubling Your Money

Ever wondered if there's a sneaky math trick that can show you how fast your money can double without having to perform complex calculations? Well, hold onto your hats, because there's a secret math superhero called the Rule of 72, and it's about to make figuring out your financial future a lot more exciting and a heck of a lot easier. Imagine you've got a magic magnifying glass that lets you peek into the future to see how long it will take for your money to grow twofold. That's essentially what the Rule of 72 does with a simple, quick calculation.

So, what's this rule all about? It's a way to estimate how many years it will take for your investment to double at a given annual fixed interest rate. You simply divide the number 72 by your interest rate, and voila, you get the number of years it will take to double your money. For example, if your savings account has an interest rate of 6%, just divide 72 by 6, and you find out that it will take about 12 years for your money to double. This rule works surprisingly well and provides a quick snapshot to help with financial planning, especially for you young investors out there looking to make the most out of your savings.

Now, how about putting this Rule of 72 into practice? Let's say you've started mowing lawns or babysitting and you're earning some money that you want to save and grow. If you put this money into a savings account with an interest rate of 3%, according to the Rule of 72, it would take 24 years to double (72 divided by 3 equals 24). But if you find another way to invest that money at a 9% return, it would only take 8 years to double (72 divided by 9 equals 8). This exercise not only helps in understanding how the rule works but also shows the impact of higher interest rates on your savings growth over time.

Let's turn this concept into a fun, interactive learning session. Imagine setting up a simulation game where you manage a virtual investment portfolio. You start with a certain amount of virtual money, choose different interest rates to apply to your investments, and then use the Rule of 72 to see how long it would take for each investment to double. This game could be played on paper, a computer, or even as a mobile app, making it accessible and engaging. You'd make decisions on how to allocate your funds across different investments with varying interest rates, and watch as the Rule of 72 shows you the potential growth over time. This not only cements your understanding of the rule but also sharpens your strategic thinking about investments and patience.

By embracing the Rule of 72, you're equipped with a handy tool that demystifies the growth of investments and serves as a constant reminder of the value of patience. It's a straightforward yet powerful way to visualize the future potential of your savings and can be a game-changer in how you plan and manage your financial resources. So next time you save some money, remember the Rule of 72, and let those numbers inspire you to keep saving and planning for bigger and better returns.

Financial Goal Setting: Making Dreams a Reality

Have you ever daydreamed about building the ultimate treehouse in your backyard or owning that super cool, shiny bicycle that you saw in the store window? Well, setting financial goals isn't just about dreaming big—it's about making those dreams a reality, step by manageable step. This is where SMART goals swoop in to save the day, turning your lofty dreams into achievable milestones. SMART stands for Specific, Measurable, Achievable, Relevant, and Time-bound. Each element of a SMART goal helps ensure that your financial target isn't just a wish upon a star, but a well-defined target with a clear plan of action.

Let's break it down with a fun example. Imagine you want to buy a new gaming console. A SMART goal for this might look something like this: "I want to save $300 to buy a new gaming console in six months by saving $50 from my monthly allowance." See how specific and clear that is? You know exactly how much you need, what you're saving for, and how long you have to achieve it. This clarity is like having a roadmap for a treasure hunt—it guides you where you need to go without getting lost in the distractions of other spending temptations.

Now, dreaming big and planning smart is all about balancing what you want now with what you want most. Encourage kids to think about both short-term and long-term goals. Short-term goals might be things they can achieve within a few months, like buying a new skateboard or saving for a special concert. Long-term goals require more patience and persistence, such as saving for college or buying their first car. This distinction helps kids not only prioritize their savings but also gives them a taste of gratification at different intervals—quick wins in the short term and major achievements in the long run.

But where does all the money for these goals come from? That's where the crucial role of saving and investing comes into play. Think of saving as your safe, steady companion in the journey toward your financial goals. It's reliable and relatively risk-free, but it grows slowly. Investing, on the other hand, is like the adventurous friend who might know ways to make your money grow faster, though sometimes taking risks is part of the journey. Both saving and investing are important because they use different approaches to help you accumulate the funds needed to achieve your goals. Regular savings accounts are great for short-term goals, while investing might be better suited for long-term goals, where the extra time can help smooth out the risks and bring greater growth opportunities.

Keeping track of your progress towards these goals can be incredibly motivating. It's like watching your favorite player score points in a game—the closer they get to winning, the more exciting it gets. Tools like financial journals, mobile apps, or even a simple chart on your wall can help you and your kids see how your savings are growing. You could set up a monthly check-in to review how much you've saved, discuss what's working, and adjust your plans if need be. Visual charts are particularly effective for younger kids because they provide a clear, tangible representation of progress. Each time they add money to their savings, they can fill in a bit more of their chart, which visually reinforces the growth of their funds. This not only teaches them about the value of money and the impact of consistent saving but also builds their confidence and excitement as they see themselves getting closer to their goals.

By integrating these practices—setting SMART goals, balancing short-term and long-term aspirations, understanding the roles of saving and investing, and tracking progress—you're not just teaching kids how to manage money; you're empowering them to take control of their financial future. This proactive approach to financial goal setting helps demystify the process of achieving big dreams, making it accessible, manageable, and, most importantly, doable. So next time your kids have a big dream, sit down together, craft a SMART goal, and start taking those small, determined steps towards making it a reality. After all, every big achievement starts with the decision to try, and with these tools in hand, there's no limit to what you and your young dreamers can accomplish.

<u>Money Challenges for Kids: Fun Ways to Learn Saving and Investing</u>

Let's spice up the way we think about money management. Instead of viewing saving and investing as mere chores, imagine turning them into exciting challenges and games. Just like your favorite video game, where each level tests a different skill, setting up money challenges can be an exhilarating way to boost your financial prowess. Think about it—money management could become as engaging as building the highest score or beating the toughest boss!

So, how about starting with creating money challenges? Here's a fun idea: set a challenge to save a small amount of money each week. It could be something as simple as saving spare change from purchases or setting aside a dollar every Sunday. To ramp up the fun, turn it into a visual game. Create a chart or a savings tracker and mark each week's savings goal with a different color. As each week passes, color in the amount saved. It's like filling in a rainbow, where each color represents a step closer to your savings pot of gold. This visual representation not only makes the challenge more tangible but also adds an element of artistry and game-play to saving.

Now, let's blend learning with some good old board game fun. Financial board games or online simulations are fantastic tools for teaching money management, saving, and investing principles in an interactive setting. Games like 'The Game of Life' or 'Monopoly' have versions that focus specifically on financial decisions, allowing players to navigate through various investment and savings scenarios. These games provide a safe and fun environment to make financial decisions, see the consequences of those decisions, and strategize better moves. The competitive element of trying to win the game by making smart financial choices adds an extra layer of engagement.

Peer challenges add another dimension to learning about money. Organize a group challenge with friends or family members where everyone sets a personal savings or investment goal. Each participant tracks their progress and shares updates at regular family meetings or get-togethers. This not only fosters a sense of community and support but also encourages learning from each other's experiences and strategies. You could create a chart that tracks everyone's progress and display it in a common area, turning saving into a shared mission where everyone cheers each other on.

Finally, rewarding achievements in these challenges can significantly reinforce positive financial behaviors and learning. When a child reaches a savings goal, celebrate it with a meaningful reward. This could be a small treat, an extra hour of playtime, or a special outing. The key is to make the reward something that truly resonates with the child, making the achievement feel celebrated and valued. This not only boosts motivation but also helps associate positive feelings with financial success, encouraging a healthy and proactive attitude towards managing money.

These fun and educational challenges transform the concept of financial management from mundane to exhilarating, making saving and investing not just a habit, but a favorite activity. By integrating these challenges into regular routines, kids learn crucial financial skills in a manner that's engaging and memorable, setting the foundation for a lifetime of smart money management.

And with that, we wrap up our exploration into making saving and investing a thrilling part of every kid's life. From understanding the power of interest in growing your money to setting and achieving big financial goals, this chapter has equipped you with the tools to turn those first saving steps into a full-blown sprint towards financial savvy. As we continue on, remember, every dollar saved or invested is like a seed planted today, growing into the financial security and freedom of tomorrow. Ready for the next adventure in our financial literacy quest? Let's keep the momentum going!

Chapter 4: Money in the Digital Age

Remember the good old days when piggy banks and dollar bills ruled the roost? Well, times have changed, my friends! Today, we're navigating a landscape where digital dollars and electronic wallets are becoming as common as those old-school metal coins we still find under couch cushions. Let's embark on a digital money adventure, where we'll decode everything from online banking to the nifty gadgets that make spending and saving as easy as clicking a button. So buckle up, because we're about to take a turbo-charged ride into the future of money!

Understanding Digital Money: From Banks to Apps

Evolution to Digital Money

Picture this: just a few decades ago, if you wanted to buy a comic book or a candy bar, you'd pull a crumpled bill out of your pocket or dig through your backpack for some spare change. Fast forward to today, and money has taken on forms that our grandparents would've found more mysterious than a magic trick. Digital money, my young padawans, is the new star of the financial universe. But how did we get here?

It all started with the basics—coins and paper money. But as technology evolved, so did the ways we handle our moolah. Enter checks, credit cards, and eventually, electronic transfers, which allowed us to move money without ever touching it. Mind-blowing, right? Now, we've got digital wallets on our smartphones and watches. Just a tap, and you've paid for your pizza or downloaded your favorite game. This transformation didn't just happen overnight; it built upon centuries of trust and innovation in how we view and exchange value.

Each step, from gold coins to tapping your phone to pay, has been about making transactions easier, faster, and more secure.

How Digital Transactions Work

Now, let's unravel the magic behind digital transactions. Imagine you want to buy a new skateboard from an online store. You select the raddest one, hit the 'pay now' button, and boom—transaction completed. But what happens in the digital backstage? When you make that purchase, your payment goes through a series of super-secure electronic checks and transfers. It zips from your bank or credit card, through a network that makes sure the money is good, and lands in the store's account, all quicker than you can say "radical!" This digital dance happens via the internet, using sophisticated systems to ensure that every penny goes exactly where it should. It's like having an invisible financial butler who takes your money and hands it politely to the seller.

Different Types of Digital Money

In the digital age, money comes in several trendy outfits. There's the classic online bank account, where you can manage your money without ever walking into a physical bank. Then there are mobile wallets like Apple Pay or Google Wallet, where your smartphone becomes your wallet, holding digital versions of your cards. And let's not forget about prepaid cards—these are like gift cards you can use almost anywhere, pre-loaded with cash for you to spend. Each of these options offers its own mix of convenience and security, giving you the power to choose how you want to interact with your money in the digital world.

Safety First

But with great power comes great responsibility, right? The digital world is amazing, but it's also like the Wild West, with hackers and cyber bandits lurking around. That's why security is the name of the game. Encryption—think of it as secret code for your financial information—keeps your money safe as it travels across the internet. Secure connections, like those starting with 'https' in your web browser, act as armored vehicles for your transactions. And just like you wouldn't share your secret diary, keeping your passwords and PINs safe is crucial. Always remember, in the digital world, being aware and cautious is your best armor.

Navigating this digital money landscape might seem daunting, but it's also incredibly empowering. With a few taps, you can manage your savings, make purchases, and even track your spending from anywhere in the world. It's like having a financial command center in your pocket, giving you the freedom and tools to make smart money choices in a connected world. So, as we continue this journey through the digital age of money, think of yourself as a pioneer, exploring new territories and harnessing the power of technology to take control of your financial future. Let's keep this adventure going, learning and adapting as we go, and who knows? Maybe you'll be teaching your parents a thing or two about digital dollars and smart spending!

<u>Using Technology to Manage Money: Tools and Apps</u>

Imagine your smartphone or tablet as a digital Swiss Army knife. Just as the classic tool flips open to reveal scissors, a knife, or a screwdriver, your device can unlock a treasure trove of apps specifically designed to manage money smarter and more effectively. Let's dive into this digital toolbox and explore how these modern marvels can turn you and your young financiers into budgeting wizards, savings gurus, and goal-setting champions.

First up, we have financial management apps that are perfect for keeping track of allowances, savings, and even spending. Think of apps like 'Bankaroo' or 'iAllowance' as your personal finance assistants. They work by giving kids (and parents) an easy way to see where their money is coming from and where it's going. For instance, every time your little one completes a chore, a predetermined amount of money gets added to their virtual balance in the app. Want to save up for that new video game or maybe a cool new bike? These apps let you set specific savings goals and show your progress in fun, engaging ways, like filling up a digital piggy bank or watching a savings tree grow leaf by leaf. The beauty of these tools lies in their ability to make abstract concepts tangible, helping kids visualize their financial achievements in real-time.

Now, let's talk about budgeting tools that bring a dash of color and excitement to what might otherwise seem like a dull task. Apps like 'Ynab' (You Need A Budget) or 'Mint' provide platforms where you can create budgets that are as vibrant and dynamic as a video game dashboard. They allow you to allocate specific amounts for different categories like snacks, games, or savings. What's really cool is that they often use graphs and charts, which kids can customize with different colors and labels, making the budgeting process visually appealing and easier to grasp. As expenses are logged, these apps update the charts, providing a clear picture of where money is being spent and how much is left for other uses. It turns the act of budgeting into a visual and interactive experience that not only teaches valuable financial skills but also keeps everyone engaged in the process.

Setting and monitoring financial goals is another superpower these apps bestow. Whether it's saving for a new skateboard or setting aside money for a family outing, these tools help set clear, achievable targets. They break down your big dreams into small, actionable steps and keep track of your progress with notifications and reward animations when you hit milestones. This feature taps into the game-like experience that many kids love, turning each financial goal into a level to beat. It encourages a sense of accomplishment and teaches patience and persistence, reinforcing the concept that good things come to those who plan and persevere.

Moreover, the perks of leveraging these digital financial tools stretch beyond their entertainment value. They're super handy, allowing you to peek at balances, refresh budgets, or eye those savings targets wherever you are, straight from your gadget. The precision is spot-on, capturing every dime spent or saved in the moment, which helps dodge the slip-ups often seen with paper-and-pencil tracking. Plus, these apps are like having a financial detective by your side, uncovering clues in your spending habits to reveal where you can stash away a few extra bucks or adjust behaviors for a healthier wallet. This instant feedback loop and the flexibility to tweak things as life happens position these digital aids as essential sidekicks in the daily dance of dollar management and future financial dreaming.

Incorporating these digital tools into your financial education efforts opens up a world where managing money is not only essential but also exciting and accessible. It empowers kids and adults alike with the knowledge and skills to handle their finances with confidence, making informed decisions that pave the way for a secure and prosperous future. So, as we continue to navigate the ever-evolving landscape of money management, these tools stand as beacons of innovation and education, turning every device into a gateway to financial literacy and independence.

Online Shopping Basics: Do's and Don'ts for Kids

Ah, online shopping! It's like having a gigantic store in your living room, where you can snag a new skateboard, the latest superhero figure, or that book you've been dying to read, all with a few clicks or taps. Pretty convenient, right? But before you or your little shopper dive into the virtual aisles, let's talk shop—safely and smartly. Just as you wouldn't sprint through a physical store grabbing everything in sight, navigating online shopping requires a bit of know-how and caution.

First up, understanding how online shopping works can turn you from a browsing newbie into a savvy e-shopper. Here's the lowdown: it starts with finding what you want on a website or a shopping app. You add items to your digital cart, which is just like a real shopping cart, except it doesn't squeak or have a wobbly wheel. Once you've picked your treasures, it's time to check out. This is where you enter your payment information and choose how fast you want your goodies delivered. Then, voila, your order is on its way to your doorstep. This process isn't just about ease and convenience; it's a fantastic way to compare prices across different stores without having to trek from one end of the mall to the other. Plus, online stores are open 24/7, so you can shop in your pajamas at midnight if that's what tickles your fancy.

Now, while shopping in your PJs is a definite perk, let's ensure it's done safely. Safe online shopping practices are the guardrails on your shopping spree highway. Always start by making sure any site you shop on starts with 'https'—that extra 's' stands for secure, meaning any information you send is encrypted, keeping it safe from prying eyes. It's like sending your secret agent messages in code. Also, keep your personal info under lock and key. That means not sharing passwords or your payment details in places that aren't secure. And always, always read the return policies. Some items might not be returnable, or there could be a fee, which is important to know before you buy. It's like knowing the rules of a game before you start playing—you definitely want to know what you can and can't do.

Let's not forget the power of comparison shopping online. This can be a game-changer in getting the most bang for your buck. Websites like PriceGrabber or Google Shopping let you compare prices across multiple retailers with just a few clicks. Imagine you find that skateboard you've been eyeing up on one site. A quick search could reveal that another site offers it at a lower price, or maybe has a coupon code you could use. It's like going on a treasure hunt, where the treasure is saving money, and who doesn't love finding treasure, right?

Finally, a big part of online shopping, especially for you young folks, involves teamwork. And by teamwork, I mean shopping with a parent or guardian. It's crucial to have someone older guiding you through the process, ensuring that the sites are safe, that you're not oversharing personal information, and that your purchases are sensible. Think of them as your shopping coach, helping you make the best plays while keeping an eye out for any fouls.

Navigating the world of online shopping can be as exciting as exploring a new game level, but it's important to play it safe and smart. By understanding how it works, sticking to secure practices, mastering the art of comparison shopping, and teaming up with an adult, you can enjoy the convenience of shopping online while being a wise, well-informed consumer. So next time you're about to click 'add to cart,' remember these tips and treat the online shopping world as a fun, vast marketplace that's yours to explore, securely and confidently.

Digital Dollars: Keeping Your Money Safe Online

Navigating the digital world can sometimes feel like you're a character in a spy thriller—dodging cyber villains and protecting your treasure trove of personal information. Think of the internet as a bustling city; it's exciting and full of opportunities, but just like any big city, it has its share of risks, especially when it comes to your digital dollars. Let's talk about some of those sneaky risks like phishing, scams, and fraud, and arm you with the superhero gadgets (aka strategies) you need to protect your financial fortress.

Phishing, for instance, is not about catching fish; it's a trick used by cyber tricksters to snag your personal information. Imagine you get an email that looks like it's from your bank, asking you to log in and confirm some details. But click on that link, and boom, you've just given your password to a scam artist. These scams can dress up as anything: from a message from a friend, a tech support call, or even a sweepstakes winning! They often create a sense of urgency, like warning that your account will be closed if you don't act fast. It's all about making you click without thinking. The key is to be like a detective—always verifying the source before sharing any personal information. Teach your kids to double-check with you before responding to unexpected requests and remind them that real banks or companies will never ask for sensitive information via email or phone.

Protecting personal information is like keeping your secret superhero identity safe. Start with strong passwords. Think less '123456' and more '$uper$ecurePassw0rd123!' Encourage your kids to create passwords that are long, unique, and use a mix of letters, numbers, and symbols. Just like a secret code that only they know. And speaking of codes, two-factor authentication (2FA) is like the secret knock on the door to your digital house. It adds an extra layer of security by requiring not only your password but also something else—like a code sent to your phone—to access your account. It's like having a double-locked door where a burglar needs two keys instead of one to get in.

When it comes to making payments online, the type of payment method you choose can also play a big part in keeping your digital dollars secure. Credit cards, for instance, often offer good fraud protection, which can be a safety net if something goes wrong. Services like PayPal or digital cards specifically designed for minors can provide additional layers of security, by acting as a buffer between your bank account and the wild west of the internet. They monitor transactions for suspicious activity and can help shut down fraud before it drains your digital wallet. Teach your kids the importance of using these secure methods, and why sometimes, paying with a credit card is safer than a direct debit from a bank account, especially on new or unfamiliar websites.

Lastly, regular monitoring of financial accounts is like having a high-tech security system for your finances. Most banks and payment services offer tools to help you keep an eye on your transactions, often in real time. Set up alerts so that you get a message whenever there's a new transaction. It's like having a watchdog that barks whenever someone opens the financial gate. Encourage your kids to regularly check their savings accounts or any digital wallets they use. Make it a routine, perhaps once a week, to sit down together and review the transactions. Not only does this help catch any fishy activity early, but it also provides a great opportunity to discuss spending habits and financial planning, reinforcing the principle of mindfulness in managing money.

Navigating the digital financial world safely is about being aware, prepared, and proactive. By understanding the risks, using the right tools, and keeping a vigilant eye on accounts, you and your kids can protect your digital dollars and enjoy the benefits of the online financial world without falling victim to its pitfalls. So, remember, in the digital age, being a smart and safe user is just as important as being a savvy saver or shopper. Let's keep those cyber villains at bay and turn the internet into a safe playground for your digital dollars!

The Future of Money: What Lies Ahead?

As we skate into the future, the landscape of money and how we interact with it is zooming towards some pretty sci-fi realms. Imagine a world where paying for your arcade tokens or that neon-green skateboard is as simple as a smile at a scanner or a wave of your hand. Financial technology, or fintech, as the cool kids call it, is rapidly morphing, bringing us not just new gadgets and apps but entirely new ways to think about and handle our dough. So, let's peek into this crystal ball and explore some of the electrifying trends and predictions shaping the future of our financial universe.

Trends in Financial Technology

Right now, fintech is like a high-speed train, and we're all aboard! Mobile banking is one car of this train, and it's packed. It's not just about checking your balance anymore; you can now send money, invest, or even apply for loans—all from your phone. Then there's contactless payment—tap-and-go technology. You've probably seen folks tapping their cards or phones on a reader to buy a smoothie or movie ticket. It's quick, it's sleek, and it's becoming more common by the day. But hang on, because there's more—artificial intelligence (AI) is joining the fintech party too. AI is helping banks and apps get smarter about helping you manage your money. They can analyze your spending habits, nudge you about bills, or even suggest ways to save. It's like having a financial advisor in your pocket, one that learns and grows with you.

The Role of Technology in Financial Accessibility

One of the most heartwarming parts of this tech revolution is how it's opening doors for everyone around the globe to step into the financial world. Technology is democratizing financial services, making them accessible in far-flung rural areas or for folks who've traditionally been left out of the banking system. Mobile money services, where people can send and receive money using just their phones, are transforming economies in places like Africa and Asia. These services are not just convenient; they're life-changing, offering people security, privacy, and control over their finances. It's a powerful reminder of how technology can do more than just make life easier or more fun; it can make it profoundly better.

Predictions for Future Money

Now, let's rev up our time machines because the future of money holds some thrilling possibilities. Biometric security is one of the biggies. Imagine using your fingerprint, your eyes, or even your heartbeat to authorize transactions. No more forgotten passwords or hacked accounts—just you, being uniquely you, unlocking your financial world. Then there's blockchain technology, which you might have heard about in the context of cryptocurrencies like Bitcoin. But it's much bigger than just digital currencies. Blockchain offers a way to securely and transparently handle all kinds of transactions, from buying a car to voting in elections. It could revolutionize not just how we use money but how we interact with the systems and institutions that shape our world.

Preparing for Changes

With all this high-tech wizardry on the horizon, how do we prepare? Staying informed and adaptable is key. The world of fintech is evolving at warp speed, and it's crucial to keep up. This doesn't mean you need to be a tech whiz or a financial guru; it just means being open to learning and evolving. Encourage curiosity and a love of learning in your kids. Explore new apps together, read up on emerging technologies, or even attend a workshop or two. Think of this as building your financial toolkit for the future—a toolkit that will help you navigate new developments and seize opportunities as they arise.

Diving into the future of money, we're not just looking at changes; we're looking at transformations that will redefine how we interact with money, making it more integrated with our digital lives than ever before. Whether it's through smarter apps, wider accessibility, or groundbreaking security measures, the future promises to make managing money easier, safer, and more inclusive. And as we move forward, embracing these changes with open arms and curious minds will not only help us keep pace with the times but also empower us to take control of our financial destinies in this brave new digital world.

Cryptocurrencies: A Kid-Friendly Introduction

Hey, have you ever wondered about this buzzword "cryptocurrency" that seems to pop up everywhere from news headlines to conversations at your local coffee shop? Well, strap in because we're about to take a whirlwind ride into the world of digital treasure known as cryptocurrencies. Think of them as the modern-day pirate's loot, but instead of gold coins, they're digital coins!

So, what are cryptocurrencies exactly? In simple terms, cryptocurrencies are types of digital or virtual money. Unlike the dollars or coins that jingle in your pocket, cryptocurrencies don't have physical forms. Instead, they live online and use cryptography (that's a fancy term for secret coding) to secure their transactions. Imagine sending secret, coded messages to your friends where no one else can read them; that's kind of what happens with cryptocurrency transactions. They're secure, which means only the sender and receiver know what's up with the money being moved around.

Now, let's dive a bit deeper into how these digital coins work. The secret sauce behind cryptocurrencies is something called blockchain technology. Think of blockchain as a magical book that records every single transaction of a cryptocurrency, like a diary that keeps track of every penny spent or received. Each page in this book is called a "block," and once a page is filled with transactions, it's added to the chain of previous pages or blocks. What's super cool is that once something is written in this magical book, it can't be erased or changed—making it a super secure way to keep track of transactions. This transparency and security are what make cryptocurrencies pretty unique as a form of money.

Let's talk about some famous cryptocurrencies you might have heard of: Bitcoin and Ethereum. Bitcoin, the granddaddy of them all, was the first cryptocurrency and is still the most well-known and widely used. It's like the Coca-Cola of digital currencies. Then there's Ethereum, which is sort of like Bitcoin's younger, tech-savvier sibling. It doesn't just handle currency transactions but can also be used to create and manage 'smart contracts'—contracts that automatically execute themselves when certain conditions are met, without needing a middleman like a lawyer. Cool, right?

But as awesome as cryptocurrencies sound, they come with their own set of challenges. One of the biggest is their volatility. Just like the seas can change from calm to stormy, the values of cryptocurrencies can swing wildly from high to low in no time. This can make them a risky choice for investing your hard-earned money. Also, because they're relatively new and operate outside of traditional banking systems, they're not as regulated, which can be a bit like the Wild West—exciting but also a bit risky.

In wrapping up our crypto journey, it's clear that cryptocurrencies are not just a fleeting trend—they're a fascinating part of our digital future. They offer a peek into a world where money is not just something you hold in your hand, but a dynamic, secure, and global form of currency that transcends traditional boundaries. As we keep our eyes on these digital treasures, understanding them becomes not just fun but necessary. They teach us about the evolution of money, the importance of security in digital transactions, and the exciting possibilities that technology holds for our financial future. So, whether you decide to become a cryptocurrency guru or just enjoy knowing about this cool digital cash, you're now equipped with the knowledge to dive deeper into the ever-evolving world of money. Let's keep our curiosity sparked and our minds open as we sail into the vast, uncharted waters of the digital age of finance!

Chapter 5: Responsible Money Habits

Think back to the last time you found an extra dollar in your pocket—it felt like winning a mini lottery, right? Now, imagine if you could turn that surprise and joy into a powerful lesson about giving and sharing. In this chapter, we're going to explore how money isn't just a tool for buying that latest gadget or snack—it's also a magical key that can unlock generosity, impact lives, and even transform communities. Let's dive into how you, the superheroes in your kids' lives, can guide them to use their financial powers for good!

<u>Giving and Sharing: The Role of Money in Helping Others</u>

When we think about money, it's often about earning, saving, or spending. But there's a super special aspect of financial savvy that doesn't get enough limelight—giving. Why is giving important, you ask? Imagine a world where everyone shares a slice of their pie, no matter how big or small. This sharing does more than just fill bellies; it creates a ripple of kindness and support that can spread through communities, making them stronger and happier. Teaching kids the importance of charitable giving instills a sense of empathy and responsibility. It shows them that their actions, no matter how small, can make a big difference.

Let's break down some ways kids can dive into giving. Donating a portion of their allowance is a great start. Whether it's a dime or a dollar, setting aside a little money each week or month can add up to a generous donation to a cause they care about. But giving isn't just about money; it's also about time and effort. Kids can engage in fundraising activities, like bake sales or craft fairs, where proceeds go to local shelters or global relief funds. Or, they can participate in charity drives at school, collecting everything from canned foods to warm coats for those in need.

Now, you might wonder, does giving a few coins or helping in small ways truly make a difference? Absolutely! Let's consider a case where a group of kids organized a lemonade stand to raise money for a local animal shelter. By the end of the day, not only did they quench the thirst of dozens of neighbors, but they also raised enough money to help feed the shelter animals for a month. This example shows that when kids contribute to a cause, the impact can be substantial. It turns abstract numbers into tangible results, like meals for furry friends or books for fellow students.

Encouraging empathy through giving is perhaps one of the most profound lessons in financial literacy. When kids see how their contributions help others, they learn to connect money with emotions and societal impact. They understand that their financial decisions, even as children, can echo throughout their community and beyond. This realization fosters a deeper appreciation for what they have and nurtures a willingness to help others. Through giving, children not only become more financially wise but also grow as compassionate and empathetic individuals, ready to take on the world not just as savers or spenders, but as givers.

So, as we continue exploring responsible money habits, remember that teaching kids about money is also about guiding them to use their financial resources to make positive changes. It's about showing them that their piggy banks can be powerful tools for good, turning every saved coin into a stepping stone towards a kinder, more generous world. Let's encourage our young ones to open their hearts as they open their wallets, and watch as they grow into not just financially savvy individuals, but also caring, globally-minded citizens.

<u>Understanding Taxes: Why We Pay and What They Do</u>

Have you ever wondered why adults often talk about taxes with a deep sigh? It might seem like a grown-up grumble, but taxes are actually more interesting than they first appear, and they affect everyone, even kids like you! Think of taxes as a subscription fee we all pay for living in our wonderful community. This "subscription" helps cover everything from keeping our parks clean and beautiful to ensuring our schools and libraries are well-equipped and cozy. Let's unwrap this concept a bit, shall we?

Taxes are a bit like the dues we pay to be part of an awesome club—the club being our country or community. Every time your parents buy something from the store, a little extra money, called sales tax, is added to the price. This might seem annoying at first—why pay more, right? But this extra bit goes into a big pot that funds various public services. For instance, when you buy that delicious ice cream from your local shop, the sales tax you pay might help fund the local zoo or repair the swings in the park you love. It's like giving back to your own community every time you make a purchase, helping to make it a better place to live.

But how exactly is this tax money collected and calculated? It's simpler than it sounds. Let's stick with the sales tax example. Say you buy a book for $10, and the sales tax rate is 10%. The total cost of the book becomes $11.

That extra buck? It's what we call sales tax. This cash zips over to the government, which then spreads it out to cover things like schools, keeping us safe, and building roads. Not everywhere charges the same amount of sales tax, and what items get taxed can also change from place to place. For instance, basic foods might not get taxed to make sure they stay affordable for everyone.

Now, why should we even care about these taxes? Well, besides keeping our streets clean and our parks green, taxes help fund bigger projects like building roads and maintaining public libraries—places where you can dive into magical worlds through books for free! They also ensure that firefighters and police officers have the equipment they need to keep us safe. So, when you see a firefighter bravely tackling a blaze, remember, it's partly those tax dollars at work!

Linking taxes to our duty towards the community may seem like a grown-up concept, yet it's essentially about recognizing how we all play a part in enhancing our community's quality of life. By paying taxes, we are all agreeing to chip in, to share the load, and to support one another. It's a way of showing that we care about our community and believe in making it a better place for everyone. And as you grow up, understanding this will help you see taxes not just as a deduction from your wallet, but as a vital contribution to the common good.

In this light, taxes are not just a financial obligation but a way of participating in community life and ensuring that everyone, regardless of their background, has access to essential services and a higher quality of life. It shows kids that being a responsible citizen doesn't start when you're all grown up; it starts now, with understanding and appreciating how our contributions, no matter how small, help shape the world around us. By learning about taxes, you're getting a sneak peek into how you can play an active role in your community, helping to maintain and improve the places you live, learn, and play.

Protecting Your Money: Avoiding Scams and Frauds

Let's talk about something a little less fun but super important - keeping your hard-earned money safe from the sneaky hands of scammers and fraudsters. Just like in those video games where you need to dodge traps and outsmart villains to protect your treasure, in real life, there are some tricks and traps you need to be aware of to keep your money safe. Scams and frauds can sometimes dress up as amazing offers or urgent requests, but with the right knowledge, you can spot these disguises and keep your treasure chest secure.

First up, let's learn how to spot these tricky scams. Imagine you're playing detective, and your mission is to uncover the truth behind some too-good-to-be-true offers. Scammers often dangle enticing carrots—like free trips, huge cash prizes, or exclusive gaming gear—for almost no effort. The catch? They often need your personal info or a small payment to unlock these 'prizes.' Red alert! Here's where your detective skills kick in. Any offer that asks for personal information like your password, account number, or requires upfront payment, especially under pressure, is waving a big red scam flag. Teach your kids to be wary of these offers and to question every detail. Why do they need your information? What's in it for them? By turning this into a game of 'spot the scam,' you make the learning process engaging and empowering.

Now, onto the superhero gear for defending against scams—preventative measures. Think of these as your personal security gadgets. One of the most powerful gadgets in your arsenal is the 'Never Share' shield. Just like you wouldn't share the secret code to your treehouse, never share your passwords, PINs, or sensitive personal information. Whether online or in real life, keep this information under wraps. Another key tactic is the 'Double-Check' binoculars. Always double-check the source of any request for your information or money. This means verifying phone numbers, email addresses, and websites by looking them up yourself instead of clicking on links provided in emails or messages. Make it a rule to discuss any financial decisions or actions with a trusted adult—a simple, effective strategy that adds an extra layer of protection.

But what if, despite your best efforts, a scam sneaks past your defenses? Here's your game plan. First, don't panic. Scammers thrive on creating urgency and fear. Take a deep breath and step back. Next, talk to a trusted adult—be it a parent, teacher, or a family friend. They can help you assess the situation and figure out the next steps. Together, you can contact your bank to secure your accounts, change passwords, and report the incident to authorities like the Federal Trade Commission or local consumer protection agencies. These steps help stop the scammers in their tracks and prevent them from targeting others. Remember, being open about the experience and discussing what happened is crucial. It's not just about rectifying the situation; it's about learning from it and strengthening your defenses for the future.

Building a careful stance towards fresh financial chances is really about developing a mindset filled with curiosity and sharp thinking. Encourage questions like, "Why is this 'free'?" or "What do they need my information for?" This is all about equipping you and your young ones with the wisdom and capabilities to thoughtfully scrutinize every scenario. It's not about sowing seeds of fear, but about fostering a sense of empowerment and sharp awareness. By understanding the signs of scams and knowing the protective measures to take, you transform potential victims into informed, empowered individuals who are tough targets for fraudsters.

Exploring how to keep your money safe may not sound as exciting as winning a video game or hitting a home run but view it as an essential skill in your adventure kit. Just as a knight sharpens their sword and a pilot checks their plane, learning to protect your money and personal information is essential. It ensures that the financial future you're working so hard to build remains secure, allowing you to focus on achieving your dreams, free from the worry of scams and frauds. So, keep these lessons in your back pocket, ready to pull out and use whenever you smell something fishy. Your financial safety net is strong, and with each lesson learned, it only gets stronger.

Ethical Spending: Buying with Conscience

Let's chat about something super cool and incredibly important—ethical spending. Imagine if every dollar you spent could do a little dance and give a high-five to the planet and its people! That's essentially what happens when you dive into the world of ethical consumption. It's all about making choices that not only satisfy your needs and wants but also consider the health of our environment and the well-being of workers around the globe. Ethical spending isn't just about buying stuff; it's about making a statement with your wallet.

Grasping the essence of ethical consumption means acknowledging that everything we buy has its own unique story. That chocolate bar from the grocery store? It starts its life as cocoa beans, often grown by farmers in distant countries. The new sneakers on your feet? They're the end product of materials sourced from multiple places and assembled by workers in factories. When we talk about ethical consumption, we're looking at this bigger picture and asking: "How were these products made? Were the workers treated fairly? What impact does this have on the environment?" It's like being a detective, but instead of solving mysteries, you're uncovering the story behind what you buy.

Making informed choices about what we buy can seem like a daunting task, but it's quite an adventure once you get the hang of it. Start by becoming a label detective. Look for labels and certifications that indicate a product is ethically sourced. For example, products with a "Fair Trade" certification mean that the producers are paid a fair wage and work under safe conditions. Similarly, items marked with "Organic" have been produced without harming the environment with excessive pesticides or GMOs. Encourage kids to look for these labels when they shop, turning each shopping trip into a treasure hunt for ethically sound products.

Supporting ethical businesses is another fantastic way to use your money for good. These are companies that go out of their way to operate responsibly, often using environmentally friendly materials and ensuring fair labor practices. By choosing to buy from these companies, you're not just getting a great product—you're also backing businesses that are committed to making the world a better place. It's like being part of a team where everyone is working towards the goal of a healthier planet and happier people.

Now, let's talk about the personal impact of these choices. It's easy to think that one person's buying decisions don't make much of a difference. But imagine what happens when you and your friends, your family, and your neighbors all start making ethical choices. Suddenly, you're not just a drop in the ocean—you're part of a wave of change. Each ethical purchase sends a message to businesses about what consumers value. This collective action can lead to significant changes in the way companies operate, pushing the entire market towards more sustainable and fair practices. So, every time you choose an ethically produced toy or piece of clothing, remember, you're voting for the kind of world you want to live in.

By embracing the principles of ethical spending, you're not just buying—you're investing in a future where the planet and its people are treated with care and respect. This approach to consumption encourages us all to think bigger and act kinder, making each purchase a reflection of our values and hopes for the world. So next time you're out shopping, take a moment to think about the power of your choices and how you can make them count for more than just the goods you take home.

<u>Financial Responsibility: What Does it Mean for Kids?</u>

Imagine if every decision you made with your money today could send a ripple through time, affecting not just your weekend plans, but also your big dreams for the future. That's the superpower of financial responsibility—it's about making choices that aren't just good for now, but that also pave the way for a rock-solid financial future. So, let's unwrap this idea and see how nurturing these skills early can turn your young ones into financial superheroes, equipped to handle whatever money challenges come their way.

Managing money wisely is like being the captain of your ship in the vast sea of financial decisions. It involves navigating through the temptations of impulsive spending and steering towards the safe harbors of saving and wise investing. But how do you instill this sense of careful navigation in kids? Start simple. Introduce them to the concept of budgeting with fun projects—maybe planning a family movie night or organizing a small party with friends. Give them a set budget and let them make decisions on what snacks to buy or which movie to rent within that budget. This hands-on approach turns abstract concepts into real, manageable practices. It teaches them to assess their choices, consider their resources, and plan accordingly. They learn that sometimes, opting for a less expensive snack means they can splurge on a better movie, balancing out their spending to maximize their enjoyment without breaking the bank.

Moving on to the long-term consequences of financial decisions, it's crucial to help kids understand that what seems like a small choice today can have big repercussions tomorrow. For instance, consistently spending all their allowance or birthday money the moment they get it can mean missing out on something really cool later on, like a new game or a special trip. Use stories or scenarios to paint a picture of how saving a little bit from each allowance could lead to them affording something much more significant and enjoyable in the future. You could even set up a simple savings tracker, where they can visually see their money growing towards their goal, making the abstract concept of "future benefits" much more tangible and understandable.

Now, let's talk about the values of accountability and honesty in financial dealings. These are the anchors that keep our financial ship stable in turbulent waters. Teaching kids to be honest about their financial habits involves open discussions about money. Have regular family 'finance meetings' where everyone talks about their spending, saving, and any challenges they might be facing. Encourage honesty by being non-judgmental and supportive, creating a safe space for kids to admit mistakes, like maybe spending their saved money on impulse buys. Discuss these slips openly, brainstorming ways to avoid similar mishaps. This not only teaches accountability but also reinforces that everyone makes mistakes, and what's important is learning from them and moving forward.

Lastly, the power of role models in shaping young minds can't be overstated. Kids often mimic the behaviors they see. So, why not introduce them to stories of individuals known for their financial wisdom? These could be historical figures, characters from books, or even members of the community. For instance, talk about someone like Warren Buffett, who started saving and investing at a very young age, or a local business owner who made smart financial choices to build their business. You can even share stories of your own financial experiences, including the good choices and the lessons learned from not-so-good ones. Showcasing real-life stories of smart money management can motivate kids to develop similar practices and grasp the real-world advantages of financial wisdom.

In weaving these threads together—wise money management, understanding the impact of financial decisions, maintaining honesty and accountability, and learning from positive role models—you equip kids with a robust financial toolkit. These skills and values not only prepare them to face financial decisions with confidence but also help them build a foundation for lifelong financial stability and success. So, let's keep these conversations going, making financial responsibility an exciting and integral part of growing up, where every choice made is a step towards a secure and prosperous future.

<u>Credit Basics: Borrowing Wisely from the Future</u>

Think of credit as your financial time machine—it allows you to borrow from your future self to meet today's needs or desires. But just like any powerful tool, using it wisely is key to ensuring it helps rather than hinders your journey. Let's unpack this a bit, shall we? Imagine you're at a store, eyeing a shiny new bike that's just a bit out of your pocket money's reach. Here's where credit can swoop in to save the day, letting you ride home with that bike today, as long as you agree to pay for it over time. Sounds like magic, right? It can be, if used wisely.

Using credit wisely means understanding when and how to use it. It's perfect for emergencies or significant, well-planned purchases. Say your family's fridge suddenly gives up the ghost. Replacing it is urgent, and using credit responsibly can be a real lifesaver, allowing your family to continue storing food safely without waiting. However, it's also crucial not to let the allure of instant gratification lead to impulsive buying. Credit is not an extension of your wallet; rather, it's a responsibility you agree to repay. This is why it's so important to plan significant purchases and ensure you have a solid plan to pay back what you owe.

Now, let's talk about the flip side—misusing credit. This can be a slippery slope. Imagine using your credit to indulge in every whim—those concert tickets, the latest smartphone, or trendy sneakers. It might feel fantastic in the moment, but it can quickly lead to a mountain of debt that's tough to climb out from under. The interest on credit means that you end up paying more than the original price of these items. If payments are missed, it could harm your financial health, affecting your ability to borrow money in the future for important things like a college loan or even a home mortgage. It's like eating too much candy—it seems like a good idea at the time, but the stomachache later isn't worth it.

Building good credit habits is crucial, and it's something you can start teaching early on. Just like any habit, the sooner it starts, the better. Teach kids the importance of timely repayment through simple examples. If they borrow money from a family member to buy something special, help them set up a repayment plan that mimics credit repayments. This could be small, manageable amounts paid back from their allowance or money earned from chores. Explain that making these payments on time is crucial, as it builds trust and reliability, just like with real credit. Also, help them understand credit terms—interest rates, minimum payments, and the total cost of credit. You can simulate these with real-life scenarios, perhaps creating a "credit contract" for a bigger allowance advance, complete with interest rates and repayment schedules.

Navigating the world of credit doesn't have to be intimidating. By understanding how to use it wisely, recognizing the dangers of misuse, and practicing good credit habits, you're setting the stage for a financially healthy future. It's about making informed choices, planning ahead, and always considering the bigger picture of your financial health. Credit, when used responsibly, can be a fantastic financial tool—just make sure you're steering it in the right direction, ensuring it benefits you in the long run.

As we wrap up this chapter on responsible money habits, remember that managing finances—whether it's giving, understanding taxes, avoiding scams, spending ethically, or using credit wisely—is all about making informed, thoughtful decisions. Each topic we've explored contributes to a comprehensive understanding of personal finance, preparing you to navigate the complexities of the financial world with confidence and savvy. Stay tuned, as our next adventure dives deeper into the exciting world of investments, where we'll learn how to grow your savings and make your money work for you!

Chapter 6: Practical Money Skills

Imagine transforming the entrepreneurial spark in your child into a blazing fire of creativity and business acumen! Welcome to the chapter where money meets imagination, and where young minds are empowered to not just think about money but to create opportunities to grow it. Here, we're not just talking about saving or spending; we're diving into the exhilarating world of mini-businesses. Whether it's a lemonade stand with a twist or a dog-walking service that offers gourmet treats for furry friends, this chapter is about turning fun ideas into profitable ventures. So, let's roll up our sleeves and turn those "What if?" dreams into "Let's do this!" realities.

<u>Planning a Mini-Business: Entrepreneurial Skills for Kids</u>

Conceptualizing a Business Idea

Every great business starts with a spark—an idea. Guiding your young entrepreneur to discover this spark involves a blend of their interests and the resources available at their fingertips. Start by brainstorming a list of things they love to do. Is your child an animal enthusiast? A pet walking service might just be their alley. Or perhaps they're a budding artist whose handmade greeting cards could brighten someone's day. Maybe it's the classic lemonade stand, but with a twist—think exotic flavors or a mobile service using a little wagon! The key here is to mesh passion with practicality. It's not just about what they love to do but also about what can feasibly be turned into a business. This initial stage is crucial because it sets the foundation for a business that not only earns money but also keeps the young mind engaged and excited.

Basics of Business Planning

Once the idea is set, it's time to lay down the groundwork. Business planning might sound daunting, but it can be broken down into simple, manageable parts. First, discuss the goals: What does your child hope to achieve? Is it about making money, gaining experience, or perhaps a bit of both? Next, tackle the budget. Start-up costs for a kid's business are usually low, but they're a great chance to introduce concepts like investment and overhead. Help them list out potential costs—materials, transportation, maybe even advertising. Then, talk about pricing. This can be a fun exercise in understanding what people might be willing to pay for their product or service. Encourage them to research by looking at what similar services cost or by asking potential customers what they'd consider a fair price. This step is not only about numbers but about beginning to understand the value of their work and time.

Marketing and Sales

Marketing doesn't have to be a series of flashy ads or complex campaigns. At its heart, it's about communication. Teach your child how to talk about their business. What makes their lemonade stand special? Why would someone choose their dog-walking service? Simple flyers, social media posts (with supervision and safety first!), or even a charming roadside sign can be effective. Then there's sales—often about making a good impression. Role-play with your child to practice how they might interact with customers. Discuss the importance of being polite, clear, and positive. Encourage them to think about what questions customers might ask and how to answer them. This not only prepares them for actual sales but boosts their confidence in speaking about their business.

Evaluating Success

Finally, every business needs to reflect on its performance. After your child's business is up and running, sit down together to review how things went. How much did they earn versus their initial goals? What feedback did they get from customers? This is a great opportunity to introduce the concept of profit and loss in a very tangible way. Discuss what worked well and what could be improved. Maybe they'll find that advertising more could bring in more customers, or perhaps tweaking their prices could increase sales. Encouraging this kind of reflection helps them learn from the experience and teaches them that running a business is an ongoing learning process.

Interactive Element: Real-Life Case Study

To bring these concepts to life, consider creating a simple case study of a child entrepreneur. For instance, detail the journey of a young person who started a handmade bracelet business. Include their initial concept, how they planned their budget, their marketing strategies, and how they evaluated their success. This real-life example can help solidify the understanding of these concepts and inspire your young reader to envision their own entrepreneurial journey.

Through these steps, you're not just helping your child start a business—you're nurturing skills like creativity, financial literacy, problem-solving, and resilience. These are invaluable tools that will serve them well beyond the lemonade stands and craft tables, equipping them with the confidence and knowledge to tackle whatever challenges and opportunities life throws their way. So, let's turn those entrepreneurial dreams into action and watch as your young business moguls learn to thrive in the exciting world of commerce.

Money Math: Fun with Numbers and Finances

Hey there! Let's turn those yawns into 'yays' with a sprinkle of fun on our number crunching adventures. Who said math has to be all about dusty chalkboards and sleepy afternoons? Not us! Today, we're diving into the thrilling world of money math, where every sum solved is a step closer to becoming a financial wizard. So, grab your calculators—or better yet, just bring your excitement—because math is about to get a major makeover in our money-savvy playground.

Practical Arithmetic Applications

Picture this: You're at your favorite candy store, and each candy is priced at 50 cents. With a couple of crumpled dollar bills in your pocket, how many can you snag before your money runs out? Here's where simple addition and subtraction come to life. You start adding up the candies, subtracting each half-dollar from your stash until you hit zero. This isn't just practice; it's practical application. Every addition or subtraction gives you a real-world outcome—more candy or less money. Now, let's say you're saving up for a new skateboard and you earn $10 a week from various chores. How long until you reach $100? A bit of division shows you need 10 weeks. That's math making your goals visible and achievable. These everyday scenarios help transform abstract numbers into tangible goals and results, making arithmetic a vital tool in your financial toolkit.

Understanding Percentages and Discounts

Next up, let's decode the mystery of percentages, especially when they sneak up in sales signs and discount tags. Imagine you're online, eyeing a video game with a flashy "25% off" banner. The original price is $40. Time for some percentage magic. Calculating 25% of $40 is like finding what one-fourth of the price is, which gives us $10. So, the sale price? Just subtract that $10 from the original price, and voila, you get it for $30! Understanding this helps you figure out whether that deal is really worth it or if you should keep your wallet snug in your pocket. And it's not just about spending less; it's about understanding how much you're really spending. This skill is especially handy during tax season or when figuring out tips at restaurants—anytime percentages pop up in your financial world.

Using Math in Budgeting

Now, let's jazz up budgeting with a dash of division and multiplication. Say your monthly allowance is $50, and you've got categories like savings, entertainment, and some must-have snacks. Deciding to save 40% of your allowance teaches you how percentages divide up your money into planned spending. Forty percent of $50? That's $20 safely tucked into savings. This leaves you with $30 to juggle between fun and food. How you allocate this teaches prioritization, planning, and stretching your financial muscles. It's not just about making ends meet but making your money meet your needs and wants efficiently.

Money Math Games

To wrap this up with a burst of excitement, let's talk games. Imagine setting up a shop where you're the cashier, and your friends or family come to buy items with play money. Each item has a price, and each buyer has a budget. They bring their items, you add up the costs, and give back the right change. This game sharpizes your addition and subtraction skills and gets you thinking on your feet, especially when there's a queue at your shop! For a digital twist, numerous apps turn budgeting and investing into thrilling challenges, where you manage virtual money to achieve goals, like building a city or traveling the world. These games not only make math fun but embed deep financial understanding through engaging, interactive play.

By weaving arithmetic into everyday spending, saving, and earning scenarios, we turn mundane math into a key player in your financial journey. Whether you're calculating discounts, dividing up your allowance, or playing shop, each number crunched is a step towards mastering your money management. So, next time you find yourself stuck with a math problem, remember: these aren't just numbers; they're the secret codes to unlocking a savvy financial future. And who knows? Maybe that next calculation you do is the one that saves you enough for that extra scoop of ice cream or gets you closer to the skateboard of your dreams.

<u>Crafting Your Own Money: Understanding Currency Design</u>

Ever held a banknote up to the light and noticed some pretty cool marks and lines that only show up in the glow? Or maybe you've tilted a bill back and forth and watched colors dance and shift? That's not just fancy artwork—it's science and security joining hands to keep our money safe and sound! Let's dive into the fascinating world of currency design, where creativity meets technology, ensuring every banknote in your piggy bank isn't just valuable; it's a mini-masterpiece of security.

Learning About Currency Features

Currency isn't just paper; it's a carefully crafted blend of art and technology designed to thwart counterfeiters. Let's start with watermarks. These are subtle images embedded into the paper itself, visible when held against light. They're like secret messages that only reveal themselves in the right light—cool, right? Then there are security threads, those shiny strips woven into the fabric of the currency, often visible on the surface and glowing under UV light. And who could forget color-shifting ink? That's the ink that changes color depending on your viewing angle. It's not just for show; it's a clever trick to make copying a bill tougher for the bad guys. These features are your money's line of defense, guarding against fraud while making sure that what you have in your wallet is the real deal.

Design Your Own Currency

Now, how about we turn you into a money designer for a day? Imagine you've been given the task to design a brand-new currency. What would it look like? Think about the value of your currency first. Will there be a $5, $10, or $20 bill? What about coins? Once you've got that sorted, think about security features. Maybe invent a watermark that represents something special about your community or a color-changing element that features your favorite colors. And let's not forget about the artistic elements! What symbols or images would represent your currency? Perhaps local wildlife, historical figures, or iconic landmarks? This exercise isn't just great fun; it also helps you appreciate the complexity and thought that go into designing the very money we use every day.

Understanding Anti-Counterfeiting

Counterfeiting, or making fake money, is a big no-no. It's like telling a fib, but in a way that can hurt lots of people by Ever held a banknote up to the light and spotted some super cool marks and lines that only appear when it's glowing? Or perhaps you've tilted a bill and watched as colors magically shift? That's not just for show—it's where science and security team up to protect our cash! Dive into the amazing world of currency design, where creativity and technology ensure every banknote in your piggy bank isn't just valuable; it's a mini-masterpiece of protection. Currency isn't simply paper; it's a masterful blend of art and technology crafted to outsmart counterfeiters. Let's kick things off with watermarks. These are sneaky images hidden in the paper, visible only when held up to light. Imagine secret messages waiting to be discovered—pretty awesome, huh? Then there are security threads, those shiny lines woven into the note, popping under UV light. And let's not overlook color-shifting ink, the ink that changes colors as you move the bill. It's not just to dazzle; it's a clever tactic to make a counterfeiter's job a nightmare. These features are the guardians of your money, making sure what's in your wallet is genuine. Now, let's switch gears and turn you into a currency designer for a day.

Picture this: You're tasked with creating a brand-new type of money. What would it look like? Start with its value. Will you design a $5, $10, or maybe a $20 bill? What about coins? Once that's decided, think about security. Maybe you'll dream up a watermark that symbolizes something meaningful about your community or choose a color-changing feature in your favorite hues. And we can't forget the artwork! Which symbols or images would you pick to represent your currency? Maybe it's the local wildlife, historical icons, or famous landmarks. This isn't just a fun project; it's a way to understand the complexity and creativity behind the money we use daily.

Counterfeiting, or the creation of fake money, is a serious no-go. It's akin to a harmful lie, impacting many by reducing the trust and value of real money. That's why those security features we talked about earlier are crucial. They present a complex challenge for counterfeiters, making it nearly impossible to produce fake bills that can pass as real. Each feature, from the watermark to the security thread and the color-shifting ink, is a puzzle that's expensive and tough to crack. By learning about these features, you not only become able to identify a fake bill but also gain a deep appreciation for the ingenious minds who design our currency to keep the economy secure.

Currency does more than facilitate transactions; it narrates a story. Around the world, nations imbue their currency with cultural significance, celebrating their history, achievements, and values. Embark on a virtual journey through currency! You might discover New Zealand's banknotes that showcase its stunning landscapes and notable figures, or Canadian bills highlighting key national symbols and made with durable polymer. This aspect of currency design transforms each banknote into an artwork and a reflection of a nation's identity and values. It's a means for countries to share their unique stories and heritage with anyone who handles their currency, providing a window into what they cherish.

So, the next time you interact with money, pause to appreciate the detailed designs and features. Each banknote you handle is a fusion of art, security, and cultural expression, carefully crafted to ensure its protection and mirror the essence of its country of origin. Whether you're spending, saving, or simply passing it along, remember, you're part of a larger narrative. And who knows? The currency you imagine today might inspire the real money creators of the future. the value of the real money in circulation. That's why those security features we talked about are super important. They make it really tough for counterfeiters to make convincing fake money that can pass as the real thing. Each feature, from the watermark to the security thread and color-shifting ink, acts as a puzzle that's costly and difficult to solve. By understanding these features, not only can you spot a counterfeit bill if you ever come across one, but you also gain a big dollop of respect for the clever minds who design our money to keep the economy safe.

Cultural Significance of Currency Design

Money does more than just pay for things; it tells a story. Across the globe, countries infuse their currency with cultural significance, showcasing their history, achievements, and pride. Take a virtual tour around the world through currency! You might find New Zealand's banknotes that display its breathtaking landscapes and notable historical figures, or Canadian bills that feature important national symbols and are even made with a polymer that lasts longer than paper. This aspect of currency design not only makes each banknote a piece of art but also a reflection of a nation's identity and values. It's a way for countries to share their unique stories and heritage with anyone who holds their currency, offering a glimpse into what they hold dear.

So next time you handle money, take a moment to notice the intricate designs and features. Each banknote in your hand is a blend of art, security, and cultural expression, meticulously crafted to ensure its safety and reflect its home country's spirit. Whether you're spending, saving, or just passing it on, remember, you're holding a piece of a larger story. And who knows? Maybe your designs today could inspire the real money makers of tomorrow.

<u>Organizing a Community Sale: Learning by Doing</u>

Imagine the buzz and excitement of a community sale, where tables are laden with treasures from around the neighborhood—gently used books, homemade cookies, quirky crafts, and so much more. Now, picture you and your kids right in the heart of this bustling marketplace, not just as buyers, but as the masterminds behind the whole event! Organizing a community sale isn't just a fantastic way to raise funds or clean out the garage; it's a goldmine of learning opportunities, especially when it comes to practical money skills. Let's walk through the steps to turn this idea into a spectacular event that could be the talk of the town (or at least the neighborhood!).

First up, planning and coordination. This stage is where your organizational wizardry comes into play, and where your kids can learn the ropes of event management. Start by setting a date and a location that's easy for everyone to get to—maybe a local park or a school yard. Next, rally the troops! Reach out to neighbors, friends, and family members who might want to set up their own tables. Here's where your kids can practice their communication skills, maybe drafting a simple invitation or helping you make phone calls. Discuss with them how to organize the layout of the sale, where each stall will be, and how to ensure there's enough space for both sellers and shoppers. Then, there's the task of advertising. Encourage your kids to get creative—design flyers, make posts for social media, or even put up signs around the neighborhood. It's all about drawing in a crowd to ensure the sale is a success.

Handling money during the sale is where things get real. This is hands-on financial education at its best. Set up a central 'bank' where sales can be monitored, and where sellers can get change if they need it. Teach your kids how to handle cash transactions, make change, and keep track of sales. Maybe they have a notebook where they jot down each transaction, or perhaps they use a simple app to keep things organized. This experience teaches them not just about math and money handling but about trust and responsibility. Plus, watching the money pile up can be a huge motivator and a real-time lesson in economics.

Teamwork and collaboration are the glue that holds the entire event together. A community sale is like a mini-festival, and it runs smoothly when everyone works together. Assign roles based on interest and age. Perhaps one child is in charge of greeting visitors, while another manages the 'bank.' Someone else might be responsible for helping sellers set up their tables. This division of labor isn't just about keeping things orderly; it's a lesson in teamwork, leadership, and cooperation. Discuss with your kids how each role is important and how working together is what makes the event successful. Encourage them to solve problems together, whether it's figuring out how to fit an extra table into a tight spot or deciding what to do if it starts to rain.

Lastly, the real-world transactions that occur during a community sale are invaluable learning experiences. They aren't simulations or hypotheticals; they're real deals happening in real-time. This authenticity makes the learning stick. Kids are not just playing shop; they're actually selling, bargaining, and managing finances. After the sale, sit down with them to go over what went well and what could be improved for next time. How much did they earn? What was the best-selling item? Did they notice any buying trends? This reflection turns experience into wisdom, providing practical insights that can be applied in future financial endeavors.

Organizing a community sale offers a dynamic way to educate children about money, business, and community engagement. It's about so much more than just making sales; it's about making connections, learning practical skills, and understanding the value of teamwork and planning. So, as you consider your next family project, think about the humble community sale—it just might be the perfect blend of fun, learning, and community spirit.

<u>Role-Playing Different Money Roles: Interactive Learning</u>

Imagine turning your living room into a bustling marketplace or a bank where the currency is fun, and the stakes are candy bars or extra screen time! Introducing kids to the concept of role-playing different money roles can be one of the most dynamic ways to teach financial literacy. It's like dressing up for Halloween, but instead of just collecting candy, they're collecting valuable life skills. Let's set the stage for a series of role-playing scenarios where children can step into the shoes of a banker, a shopper, or even a restaurant owner.

Setting up these scenarios can be as simple or elaborate as you like. Use props like play money, homemade menus, or crafted items they can "sell." The kitchen can transform into a restaurant where one child is the chef and another is the customer, or the backyard can turn into a marketplace. Here, one kid can be a banker, issuing loans to others who want to start their own 'businesses' selling crafts or snacks. These setups are not just play; they're platforms for real learning. Kids in the role of a banker need to decide who gets a loan based on their business plans, while those playing customers learn to make choices based on the money they have.

As children dive into these roles, they encounter a variety of challenges that call for creative problem-solving. For instance, what happens if the 'restaurant' runs out of 'food' (materials)? How does the banker decide who to give a loan to, and what happens if someone can't 'pay' it back? These scenarios help children understand the responsibilities involved in different roles and the impact of their decisions. It teaches them about risk (choosing which business to invest in), budgeting (managing their money to afford items on the menu), and the basics of supply and demand (deciding on the price of the crafts or snacks).

These role-playing games are enriched even further by the element of interactive problem-solving. Suppose a child who has 'borrowed' play money for their stand faces a 'budget shortfall' because not many friends are buying their crafts. This scenario can lead to a discussion about how businesses adjust to changes, like lowering prices or improving their products. Or consider a game where kids need to decide how to spend their limited amount of play money at different stalls in the 'marketplace.' During these activities, children practice their bargaining skills and figure out how to evaluate the value of items. This not only enhances their ability to think critically but also strengthens their capacity to make wise decisions.

After the role-play, gathering the kids for a discussion about what they learned can consolidate these lessons. What did they find challenging? What would they do differently next time? This reflection turns a simple game into a powerful learning experience, reinforcing the lessons and giving kids the chance to express what they've learned and how they felt. These discussions can be eye-opening as children often have unique takes on how they viewed the roles and the decisions they made.

Through these role-playing activities, children don't just learn about different monetary roles and responsibilities; they live them. They're not just told about the value of money and budgeting—they experience it firsthand through play, which deepens their understanding and retention of financial concepts. It's a dynamic way to bring the sometimes abstract concepts of economics down to earth, making them accessible and engaging. So next time you're looking for a fun activity, consider setting up a mini-market or a home bank. It's a playful and profound way to teach financial literacy that feels more like fun and less like learning, nurturing skills that will help them navigate the wider world with confidence and savvy.

<u>Designing a Kid's Budget: A Practical Project</u>

Hey, let's turn that piggy bank into a powerhouse of planning and savvy spending! Crafting a budget isn't just for grown-ups with ties and briefcases—it's a super skill that can turn you into a mini-money master. So, whether you're saving up for that blockbuster video game or just trying to stretch your allowance to cover those extra treats, knowing how to plan and track your money is like having a secret weapon in your financial arsenal. Ready to dive in? Let's start by transforming those dollars and cents into a budget that makes sense!

Step-by-Step Budget Creation

First things first, let's figure out where your money is coming from. It could be your weekly allowance, cash gifts from grandma on your birthday, or maybe you've been raking leaves in the yard for some extra dough. Whatever your income sources are, let's jot them down. This is your starting point. Next up, let's take a sneak peek at where that money's flying off to. Are you spending most of it on the latest games, snacks at the corner store, or maybe those cool stickers for your skateboard? Tracking your expenses isn't just about knowing where your money is going—it's about gaining control over it.

Once you've got a clear picture of what comes in and what goes out, it's time to play around with those numbers. How much do you think you should be spending on those non-negotiables like school supplies, and how much can you afford to splurge on the fun stuff? This is where you start setting up your budget categories. But here's the kicker—not all your money should be going out. Some of it should be growing in a savings account or maybe even in that old piggy bank. This is your chance to think about what you might want in the future—maybe a new bike or a trip to that amusement park you've been dreaming about. Allocating funds for different categories helps you not just meet your current wants but also save for those big dreams.

Using Budget Tools

Now, unless you have a supercomputer for a brain, keeping track of all these details can get a bit tricky. That's where budget tools and templates come in handy. Think of them as your personal budget assistants. You can start simple with a notebook and pen, jotting down your income and expenses and doing the math as you go. Or, if you're tech-savvy, there are tons of apps out there designed just for young spenders like you. These apps can track your spending, remind you of savings goals, and even offer tips on how to manage your money better. They're like having a tiny banker right in your pocket!

Ongoing Budget Management

Here's the secret sauce to maintaining a great budget—it needs to grow as you grow. What worked for you last year might not be enough this year. Maybe you've started mowing lawns in the summer, boosting your income, or perhaps you've taken up a new hobby that's adding to your expenses. Regular check-ins on your budget are crucial. Sit down once a month with your budget book or app and review what's happening. Are you overspending in some areas? Do you have more wiggle room for fun stuff than you thought? Adjusting your budget as you go not only keeps it relevant but also teaches you flexibility and adaptation—skills that are golden in both money management and life.

Visual Element: Budget Pie Chart

To make your budget review sessions even more effective, try creating a pie chart of your expenses. This visual tool can help you quickly see which parts of your life are gobbling up your money pie. Maybe

'Entertainment' is taking a bigger slice than you realized, or perhaps 'Savings' is just a tiny sliver that needs to grow. Adjusting your spending to better match your priorities becomes a lot easier when you can see it laid out in front of you.

Crafting and managing a budget might sound like all work and no play, but it's actually a journey filled with aha-moments and growth. It's about taking charge of your financial future, one dollar at a time. And guess what? The skills you're building now are setting you up for a lifetime of money savvy—no matter how big those dreams of yours get. So keep at it, young budgeter! Your future self will thank you.

As we wrap up this chapter on practical money skills, remember, each tool and technique we've explored is a stepping stone towards becoming a master of your financial universe. From launching your own mini-business to crafting a smart budget, you're not just learning about money—you're learning how to make it work for you. Next up, we're diving deeper into the world of investments where your money doesn't just grow—it multiplies. Get ready to turn those savings into earnings as we explore the exciting world of investing for kids. Stay tuned, because your financial adventure is just getting started!

Chapter 7 Financial Challenges and Solutions

A h, the sweet siren song of the checkout line—where last-minute candies and shiny trinkets try to jump into your shopping cart. Who hasn't been there, right? Navigating the aisles with a determined list, only to be waylaid by an impulse buy that seems just too good to pass up. We've all been caught in the whirlwind of impulse buying, and trust me, it's a breeze that blows just as strong for kids—especially when they're confronted with the latest toys or a shelf of sugary treats. But fear not! This chapter is all about arming you and your young shoppers with savvy strategies to combat those spendy temptors and turn every shopping trip into a masterclass in financial self-control.

<u>Overcoming Spending Temptations: Tips and Tricks</u>

Understanding Impulse Buying

First off, let's tackle the beast: impulse buying. It's that moment when you or your kiddo buys something without planning to—it wasn't on the list, it wasn't budgeted for, but boy, did it seem irresistible at the moment! Whether it's a toy that they just "had to have" or a snack that magically calls their name, impulse buying is often driven by emotions rather than need. It's like being on a treasure hunt where everything shiny looks like gold, but not everything that glitters is worth the coin. Recognizing this pattern is step one. Talk with your kids about how stores are designed to tempt us—the toys at eye level, the candy strategically placed at the checkout counter. Awareness is your first shield against impulse buys.

Delay Tactics

Now, for the clever bit: delay tactics. This is a super strategy where you teach your kids to hit the pause button. Here's the play: when you or your little one spots something tempting, instead of dropping it in the cart, take a moment. Maybe set a timer on your phone—give it 24 hours or even just the time it takes to walk around the block or finish a meal. This cool-off period helps dampen the "gotta have it now" fever and gives your child (and you!) a chance to think about whether it's really a want, a need, or just a passing whim. It's a bit like making cookies wait until they cool off—gives you a moment to anticipate and decide if you really want that treat or if maybe, just maybe, you're actually in the mood for something else.

Goal Reminders

Visual cues can be powerful motivators and reminders. Why not make saving and spending goals a visible part of your home décor? For instance, if your child is saving up for a big-ticket item like a new bike, help them create a vibrant savings chart or a cool collage that depicts their goal. Place it where they'll see it often—on the fridge, next to their bed, or on the family bulletin board. Every time they get tempted to spend on something less important, that image serves as a gentle nudge, reminding them of what they're saving for. It turns abstract goals into tangible, exciting visualizations that call out, "Hey, remember me? I'm worth waiting for!"

Rewards for Restrainthood

And here's the fun twist: rewards for restraint. Consider setting up a system where resisting the urge to splurge leads to special rewards. Not just any rewards, but ones that reinforce good behavior without necessarily involving spending. Maybe an extra hour of bedtime stories, a family game night, or the chance to pick the movie on movie night. These rewards celebrate the skill of self-control and turn the act of not buying on impulse into a victory worth cheering for. It's about weaving financial wisdom into the fabric of everyday life, making it as natural and rewarding as acing a test or scoring a goal in soccer.

Through these strategies, we transform shopping challenges into opportunities for growth, learning, and a bit of fun. It's not just about saving pennies; it's about enriching our kids' understanding of money and empowering them to make thoughtful decisions that reflect their values and goals. So next time you hit the stores, remember, every item not impulsively tossed into the cart is a win—a high-five to financial savvy and a step towards becoming a budgeting pro. Keep those goals in sight, those rewards in mind, and turn spending temptations into occasions to celebrate restraint and wisdom. Who knew being financially smart could feel so good?

Adjusting a Budget: What to Do When Expenses Change

Life, as they say, is what happens when you're busy making other plans, and this is especially true when it comes to managing money. Think of your budget as a living document, kind of like a plant. It needs regular attention and sometimes, a bit of pruning or repotting to thrive, particularly when the financial climate changes. Maybe you've just received a surprise bonus from your grandma, or perhaps, out of the blue, your bike needs major repairs. These moments require a nimble approach to your budget, and here's how you can pivot smoothly without missing a beat.

Now, recognizing when your budget needs a tweak is a bit like noticing when a plant needs water—there are telltale signs. For instance, if you find yourself repeatedly dipping into savings for regular expenses or if an unexpected windfall lands in your lap, these are clear indicators that your budget needs a reassessment. Engage your kids in this process; let them tell you when they think money matters are off track, like if they've spent their entire month's allowance in a week. It's about keeping the lines of communication open and making budget adjustments an engaging team activity rather than a tedious task.

Moving on to the concept of flexible budgeting, this is your budget's ability to stretch and bend without breaking. Imagine your budget is a rubber band. If fixed too rigidly, it might snap under pressure. But if it's flexible, it can adapt to hold as little or as much as needed without any tear. This flexibility means allocating more funds to necessary categories without completely derailing other financial goals. For example, if school fees increase unexpectedly, you might decide to cut back on entertainment expenses to compensate. Show your kids how adjusting the budget can keep their financial goals on track, even when unexpected expenses pop up. It's like adjusting sails on a boat to keep moving forward when the wind changes direction.

Then, there's the cornerstone of any good financial plan: the emergency fund. This fund acts like a financial shock absorber, cushioning you from the bumps and bruises of life's surprises. Starting an emergency fund can be a fun challenge for kids too. Perhaps they can save a small part of their allowance each week or save money from odd jobs. Over time, this fund grows and provides a sense of security, teaching them the value of being prepared. Plus, it's incredibly rewarding for kids to see their emergency savings grow; it's their own personal rescue fund, ready to save the day when needed.

Lastly, let's talk about scenario planning. This is where you can really turn budgeting into an adventure. Create different financial scenarios and walk through them with your kids. What would they do if they suddenly had to pay for a lost library book? Or if they wanted to buy a gift for a friend's birthday party? Use these scenarios to practice making budget adjustments. You could set up a mock 'budget board' at home where different scenarios and their financial impacts can be visualized with notes or stickers. This hands-on approach not only makes the concept of budgeting more tangible but also embeds important financial lessons through play and experimentation.

By embracing these strategies, you transform the concept of budget adjustment from a chore to an exciting part of money management. It becomes a dynamic tool that not only reflects current financial realities but also empowers you and your kids to take proactive steps in securing your financial well-being. So next time a financial curveball comes your way, remember, with a little creativity and flexibility, any budget can be adjusted to hit a home run.

Handling Financial Mistakes: Learning from Errors

Oh, the oops moments! We've all had them—those times when money slips through our fingers like sand, whether it's splurging on an unplanned gadget or forgetting to log a week's worth of expenses. But here's the scoop: these slip-ups, while frustrating, are not just stumbling blocks; they're stepping stones. They're opportunities wrapped in disguise, offering invaluable lessons in managing finances better. So, how do we turn these blunders into learning experiences for our young financial adventurers? Let's dive into the art of identifying mistakes, reflecting constructively, taking corrective actions, and building resilience along the way.

Understanding and identifying financial mistakes is the first step in our error-handling mission. It's like being a detective at the scene of a mystery—first, you have to figure out what went wrong. Did we blow our budget on too many movie nights this month? Did we forget to account for that annual subscription renewal? Recognizing these moments requires keeping a keen eye on our financial activities. For kids, this might mean noticing when their piggy bank feels lighter than it should or when their allowance seems to vanish too quickly. It's about creating an awareness that money needs to be monitored, just like their pet or their favorite plant. Encourage them to keep a simple money journal or use a kid-friendly finance app where they can track their spending and saving. The goal? To make financial reflection a regular part of their routine, just like homework or chores.

Once a mistake is spotted, it's time for some constructive reflection. This isn't about scolding or feeling bad about the error. No, it's about understanding why it happened. Was it a case of mistaken needs versus wants? Or perhaps a lack of planning? Discuss these moments openly, without judgment. Turn them into cozy couch conversations about money, helping kids understand that everyone—yes, even adults—makes financial missteps. What's crucial is learning from these experiences. For example, if they spent their entire week's allowance in one go, chat about how it felt when they couldn't buy something they really wanted later. These reflections help transform abstract regrets into concrete learning that sticks.

Now, let's roll up our sleeves for some corrective action. This is where we get proactive, turning our 'oops' into 'a-ha!' moments. If overspending is the issue, brainstorm together on ways to cut back for the next few weeks. Maybe swap a store-bought snack for a homemade treat, or enjoy a movie night at home instead of the cinema. If forgetfulness is the culprit, how about setting up reminders on a calendar or a special finance board in their room? Make this process fun—perhaps they could decorate their reminder tools, turning them into a craft project. Each corrective step should feel empowering, not punitive, reinforcing the idea that they have the power to fix their financial course.

Building resilience is perhaps the most valuable outcome of handling financial mistakes. It's about teaching kids that bouncing back is possible and that resilience is built through practice. Every financial mistake and every corrective action strengthens their ability to handle money wisely. It's like learning to ride a bike—every fall teaches you a bit more about balance, and before you know it, you're pedaling smoothly. Celebrate these resilience-building moments. Maybe create a 'bounce-back badge' or a resilience chart where they can add a star for every mistake they learn from. This not only boosts their confidence but also ingrains a vital life lesson: mistakes aren't the end of the road; they're just signs that point us to better paths.

Navigating through financial errors with your kids in this engaging, supportive way turns what could be discouraging moments into empowering learning experiences. It's about fostering an environment where mistakes are demystified, discussed, and dealt with constructively, ensuring that each financial faux pas becomes a building block for a savvier, more resilient young money manager. So next time a financial blunder crops up, remember, it's just another secret lesson in disguise, ready to be unraveled and understood, paving the way for smarter, stronger financial decisions in the future.

<u>Negotiating Allowances: Practical Tips for Kids and Parents</u>

Ah, the age-old dance of allowance negotiation—where kids try to stretch their fiscal wings and parents attempt to teach the value of a dollar. It's more than just a chat about money; it's a critical learning moment about value, communication, compromise, and documentation. Let's unwrap this bundle and see how transforming allowance discussions can be a mini-masterclass in life skills for your little CFOs in training.

Understanding Value

First up, understanding the value of work tied to allowances is crucial. It's about connecting the dots between the chores your kids do and the money they receive. This isn't just about making beds or taking out the trash; it's about helping them see the bigger picture of work and reward. For instance, if your child has been taking on more around the house, it might be time to discuss how their responsibilities align with their allowance. Explain that their efforts are valued and that their allowance is a reflection of their contribution to the household. This isn't just about giving them more money—it's about recognizing their growing capabilities and responsibilities. It's akin to a performance review at a job where good work is acknowledged and rewarded. This conversation can be a powerful motivator and an eye-opener for kids, showing them the tangible outcomes of their hard work.

Communication Skills

Next, let's talk about the art of communication, especially when it comes to discussing allowance adjustments. This is a fantastic opportunity to teach your kids how to express their needs and negotiate effectively and respectfully. Guide them on how to approach an allowance discussion with clear points and a calm demeanor. Role-playing can be a fun way to practice. You could play the 'bank manager' while your child pitches their case for an allowance increase. Encourage them to explain why they believe an increase is justified—perhaps they've taken on additional chores, or they're saving up for something special. Teach them to listen as well, just as they would in a real negotiation. This back-and-forth can not only make them better communicators but also more confident in articulating their thoughts and engaging in financial discussions.

Compromise and Agreement

Compromise is the bridge in any negotiation, and discussing allowances is no exception. Sometimes, your kid's initial request might not be feasible, but that doesn't mean the conversation should end there. This is the perfect moment to explore the concept of compromise. Maybe the full allowance increase they're asking for isn't possible, but a smaller increase could work if they take on an extra task each week. Or perhaps, the increase can be tied to saving a portion of their allowance for future expenses, like school supplies or gifts for friends' birthdays. This part of the discussion teaches flexibility and the importance of give-and-take, preparing them for the inevitable negotiations they'll face later in life, both in their personal and professional worlds.

Documenting Agreements

Finally, let's solidify these discussions with some good old-fashioned documentation. Creating a written agreement or chart that tracks chores, responsibilities, and allowance changes can be incredibly helpful. It doesn't have to be complex—a simple chart on the fridge or a note on a bulletin board can work wonders. This visual reminder helps keep both parents and kids accountable. It also gives your children a clear understanding of what's expected of them and what they can expect in return. Plus, it's a great way to introduce them to the idea of contracts and the importance of keeping records, skills that are valuable in both personal finance and the business world.

By tackling allowance negotiations through the lenses of understanding value, honing communication skills, mastering compromise, and documenting agreements, you're not just discussing money. You're equipping your kids with a toolkit for navigating the wider world. These discussions are miniature life lessons in economics, relationship management, and personal development, all wrapped up in conversations about whether they can earn a few extra bucks for their weekly tasks. So next time the topic of allowances comes up, dive in with enthusiasm. It's an investment in your child's future, teaching them skills that go well beyond financial literacy.

<u>Saving on a Low Income: Making the Most of Little</u>

When the budget is tighter than a new pair of shoes on a long walk, finding ways to stretch every dollar becomes less of a practice and more of an art form. Let's face it, managing finances on a limited income can feel like trying to fill a leaking bucket, but here's where we turn those leaks into features! It's all about prioritizing expenses, getting creative with cost-cutting, and adopting a mindset that sees saving as a thrilling challenge rather than a chore. This is not just about pinching pennies; it's about transforming them into a full-fledged financial strategy.

Let's start with the basics: prioritizing expenses. This is the foundation upon which your financial house is built. When funds are limited, covering basic needs isn't just important, it's essential. These are your non-negotiables—food, housing, healthcare, and education. Everything else can wait. Think of your budget like a pyramid. The base, the largest part, is for your essentials. Only once these are securely covered should you move up to the next levels—utilities, transportation, and only then, those little extras. Teaching kids this hierarchy of needs helps them understand why sometimes, despite desperately wanting that new video game or toy, it's more important to ensure there's enough set aside for groceries and rent first. It's a lesson in responsibility and prioritizing that will serve them well beyond their financial decisions.

Now, onto the fun part: creative cost-cutting. This is where you can really get your creative juices flowing. Think of it as a game where every dollar saved is a point scored. Coupons can be a gold mine for savings. Whether it's clipping them from newspapers or collecting digital codes, the savings can add up quickly and turn into a fun scavenger hunt for discounts. Then there's the art of substitution. Why buy new when used will do? Thrift stores, garage sales, and online marketplaces can be treasure troves for clothing, furniture, and even electronics. It's like going on a treasure hunt in your own community. And let's not forget about repurposing. That old jar can become a new vase, and those worn-out jeans? Hello, stylish new shorts! Teaching kids to see potential in what they already have not only saves money but also sparks creativity and innovation.

Incremental saving techniques are your secret weapon. When big chunks of money are hard to come by, small amounts can still pave the way to financial stability. Encourage setting aside a tiny amount regularly, no matter how small. It could be as simple as saving loose change in a jar or rounding up purchases and saving the difference. Over time, just like drops in a bucket, these small savings can fill up and even overflow. Show kids how setting aside just a dollar a week can grow over a year. It's not just about the final sum; it's about building the habit of saving consistently, turning it into a normal part of life, as routine as brushing teeth.

Lastly, the value of resourcefulness cannot be overstated. In a world that often encourages consumption, being resourceful is both a financial necessity and a valuable life skill. It's about making the most of what you have, whether it's reusing leftovers to create new meals or fixing a broken toy instead of buying a new one. This mindset turns challenges into opportunities and scarcity into innovation. It teaches kids that resourcefulness is not just about saving money; it's about fostering independence, creativity, and self-reliance. Plus, it can be a whole lot of fun to see what new things you can create with a little imagination and a lot of determination.

Navigating a tight budget doesn't have to be a downer. It's an opportunity to instill values of thrift, creativity, and perseverance in your kids. By prioritizing expenses, getting creative with savings, adopting incremental saving habits, and embracing resourcefulness, you're not just surviving on a low income; you're thriving, showing your kids that financial constraints aren't barriers but springboards to becoming more innovative, determined, and financially savvy. So, embrace the challenge, get creative, and watch as those small savings start to add up, proving that even when funds are low, your family's financial ingenuity can soar high.

<u>Creative Fundraising Ideas for Kids</u>

Ah, fundraising—when kids go from being cute to being cute and cunning for a cause! Whether it's raising money for a school trip, a community project, or a charity they're passionate about, fundraising can teach kids about money, compassion, and entrepreneurship all rolled into one. Think of it as their first dip into the world of business, but instead of profit, the real payoff is the joy of helping others and the thrill of working together towards a common goal. Let's explore some fun and creative ways to turn your little go-getters into fundraising phenoms.

Event-Based Fundraising

Picture this: a sunny day, a line of cars, and a bunch of enthusiastic kids armed with sponges and soap—a car wash fundraiser! Or how about a bake sale where cookies and cupcakes turn into cash for a good cause? Event-based fundraising is all about bringing people together and adding a little fun to the mix. These events not only raise money but also awareness for whatever your kids are passionate about. They're perfect for team building and can be a blast to organize. Think themed fun runs where every lap completed contributes a few dollars to the cause. Or a community fair where each game played or item sold adds to the fundraising pot. The key is to keep it fun, keep it safe, and keep everyone engaged. And remember, the messier the event (hello, pie-eating contest!), the more memorable it usually is.

Skill-Based Fundraising

Now, let's tap into those unique talents with skill-based fundraising. Does your child love to paint? Host an art class! Is piano more their style? How about a mini-concert for family and friends, with admission fees going to their chosen cause? This kind of fundraising not only raises money but also boosts kids' confidence in their abilities. It's about showcasing their skills and hard work, all while doing some good in the world. Plus, it gives them a taste of what it's like to use their talents professionally, which is pretty cool at any age. Whether it's teaching younger kids how to throw a perfect pitch or knitting scarves to sell at a local craft fair, skill-based fundraising encourages kids to develop and share their abilities in a way that benefits others.

Online Fundraising Platforms

In the digital age, fundraising has gone online, and it's a game-changer. Platforms like GoFundMe or Kickstarter can be perfect for older kids looking to reach a broader audience. Of course, this should always be supervised by an adult to keep everything on the up and up. Online campaigns can be incredibly effective, especially when combined with social media sharing. Help your kids put together a compelling story about their cause, perhaps with videos or photos, and watch as the donations come in from all over the globe. It's a great way to teach them about the power of community—even a digital one—and the impact of well-crafted storytelling in achieving real-world goals.

Community Service Projects

Lastly, there's the double whammy of community service projects that also act as fundraisers. Think of a neighborhood cleanup where sponsors donate for every bag of trash collected, or a read-a-thon where donations are based on the number of books read. These projects not only raise money but also improve the community and encourage active citizenship. It's about getting kids involved in bettering their world directly, seeing the immediate impact of their efforts, and understanding that fundraising isn't just about money—it's about making a tangible difference.

Through these diverse fundraising activities, kids learn a multitude of skills—from planning and organization to marketing and public speaking. But more importantly, they learn the value of teamwork, the joy of helping others, and the satisfaction of seeing a project through from idea to successful completion. Whether they're washing cars, sharing their art, reaching out to an online community, or cleaning up their local park, they're not just raising funds; they're growing as individuals and making memories that are sure to last a lifetime.

So, as we wrap up this chapter, remember, fundraising is more than just collecting money; it's an adventure in growth, learning, and community engagement. It's a chance for kids to shine, to share, and to shape their world, one dollar at a time. Get ready, get set, and let the fundraising fun begin!

Next Chapter Preview:

As we transition from the bustling world of fundraising to the next chapter, we'll delve into the nuts and bolts of setting and achieving financial goals. It's one thing to raise money, but managing it wisely? That's where true financial wisdom comes in. Stay tuned as we explore how to turn those hard-earned funds into smart money moves that make dreams come true.

Chapter 8: Building a Financially Savvy Future

Imagine you're packing for an epic adventure—a trek that will take you from the familiar trails of middle school to the uncharted terrain of high school and beyond. It's an exciting time, right? But just as you wouldn't hike a mountain without the right gear, stepping into high school without some financial know-how could leave you, well, a bit lost in the woods. So, let's load up your backpack with essential financial tools and tips that will not only help you navigate through high school but also pave the way to a financially savvy future. Ready? Let's step into the world of budgets, jobs, scholarships, and more!

<u>Planning for High School: Financial Preparation Tips</u>

Budgeting for School Needs

Navigating high school is like embarking on a grand expedition, and every explorer needs a solid plan. Start with budgeting for school-related expenses. Think about all the gear you'll need—books, supplies, and those extracurriculars that can really add up. This is where your budgeting skills come into play. Sit down with your young adventurer and map out a budget together. List out the essentials and allocate funds for each. Got a budding artist or a sports enthusiast at home? Remember to set aside something for art supplies or sports equipment.

<u>Here's a pro tip</u>: encourage your teen to contribute to their school budget. Whether it's from their allowance or a part-time job, involving them in the budgeting process not only teaches them about managing money but also gives them a sense of ownership and responsibility for

their educational journey. Plus, it's a great way to sneak in some extra math practice (don't tell them that, though).

Understanding Part-Time Jobs

As they say, there's no better teacher than experience. And what better way to learn about earning, saving, and managing money than a part-time job? Discuss the benefits of part-time work beyond the obvious paycheck—like time management, responsibility, and the sweet taste of financial independence. But it's not just about earning; it's about learning to balance work and studies. Help your teen understand how to manage their time effectively, ensuring that job hours don't collide with homework or study time.

A part-time job can be a stepping stone to bigger financial goals, too. Whether it's saving for college, a car, or even a special gadget, earning their own money can empower them to make smarter spending choices and appreciate the value of hard-earned cash.

Scholarships and Saving for College

Let's talk about making higher education more affordable - scholarships! These are like the golden tickets of the academic world, and they come in all shapes and sizes. Introduce your teen to the different types of scholarships available and how they can apply. Whether it's academic excellence, sporting prowess, or community service, there's likely a scholarship that matches their talents and interests.

But don't just stop at scholarships. Discuss the importance of saving for college early. Open a savings account specifically for higher education and explore different savings plans that can help grow their college fund. It's like planting a seed today and watching it grow into a mighty tree by the time they're ready for college.

Financial Aid Basics

Understanding financial aid is like learning a new language—it can be tricky but incredibly useful. Provide a basic overview of the different types of financial aid available, including grants, loans, and work-study programs. Explain how each type works and the implications of each choice. For instance, grants are fantastic because they don't need to be repaid, while loans do—and with interest.

This is also a great time to introduce the concept of financial literacy. Explain terms like interest rates, loan repayment plans, and the long-term impact of borrowing. It's crucial information that can help them make informed decisions about funding their education and managing any debts they might incur in the future.

Navigating the financial aspects of high school and beyond can seem daunting, but with the right tools and knowledge, it can be an empowering journey. By discussing these financial tips and strategies, you're not just preparing your kids for high school; you're setting them up for a lifetime of financial savvy. So, as they step into this exciting new phase of life, they'll feel confident and equipped to take on whatever financial challenges come their way.

Money and Friendships: Managing Social Spending

Navigating the choppy waters of social spending can feel a bit like balancing on a tightrope, especially when friends are involved. Whether it's catching the latest blockbuster, hitting up the coolest cafes, or giving the perfect gifts, managing these expenses without blowing your budget is an art form in itself. Let's unwrap some savvy strategies to keep your social life vibrant without your wallet taking a dive.

Peer Pressure and Spending

The pressure to keep up with friends can turn any savvy saver into a spendthrift. It's tough watching pals pick up the latest gadgets or fashion, and the fear of missing out (FOMO) can really make your budget bend. But here's a secret weapon: confidence in your financial choices. Start a dialogue with your young ones about the difference between wanting something because it's genuinely important to them and wanting something just to keep up with friends. Role-playing can be a game-changer here. Try out scenarios where they might feel pressured to spend and discuss ways to handle these situations gracefully. Maybe it's having a few polite but firm phrases up their sleeve, like "That sounds awesome, but I'm saving up for something big right now." It not only helps them stand their ground but also builds their confidence in making independent financial decisions.

Budgeting for Social Activities

Now, let's tackle the fun stuff: planning for outings, movies, or dining out. Here's where your budgeting skills shine. Help your kids allocate a part of their allowance or earnings specifically for social spending. This fund becomes their go-to for all things fun, giving them the freedom to enjoy outings with friends, guilt-free. But it's not just about setting the budget; it's about making it stretch. Encourage savvy spending by looking for student discounts, sharing costs like group meals, or choosing less expensive outings. Maybe instead of dining out, they opt for a picnic in the park. It's all about getting creative and making the most of every dollar, turning budgeting into a fun challenge rather than a chore.

Gift-Giving on a Budget

Gift-giving is a beautiful way to show friends you care, but it doesn't have to mean emptying your piggy bank. Encourage your kids to think outside the store-bought box. Homemade gifts, whether it's a handcrafted bracelet, a baked treat, or a personalized playlist, often hold much more meaning. Not only do they save money, but they also add a personal touch that friends cherish. Another fun idea is group gifting for a common friend. By pooling resources, everyone can contribute to a bigger, better gift without anyone breaking the bank. It's a win-win: the gift receiver gets something fabulous, and everyone saves money.

Negotiating and Compromise

When it comes to group activities, not everyone will have the same budget, and that's okay. This is a great opportunity to teach your kids about negotiation and compromise. Say the group wants to go to an amusement park, but it's a bit pricey. They could suggest alternative activities like a movie night at home or a day at a free museum. If the group still decides on the pricier option, maybe they choose a day when entry fees are discounted. Learning to negotiate and compromise not only helps keep their spending in check but also ensures that everyone in the group feels included, regardless of their budget.

By mastering these aspects of social spending, kids learn that having a great time with friends doesn't have to mean spending big. They discover the joy of being creative with their social budgets, the value of thoughtful gift-giving, and the importance of inclusive, budget-friendly fun. So, as they navigate their social worlds, they'll be equipped not just with money in their pockets but with skills that enrich their friendships and their financial savvy.

Updating Your Financial Knowledge: Staying Informed

Ah, the ever-changing world of finance! It's like a whirlwind of numbers and trends that can seem as puzzling as why the fridge light turns off when you close the door. But keeping up with financial news doesn't have to be a chore—it can be as fun and engaging as catching up on your favorite series. Think of it as tuning into the story of our economy, where each news update adds a new episode to the saga. For our young financiers, staying informed about economic trends can be both enlightening and empowering. It helps them understand the bigger picture and see how various elements of the economy connect with their own financial decisions.

Encouraging teens to follow financial news tailored for younger audiences is a great way to spark their interest. Websites and podcasts dedicated to simplifying and explaining financial news in a relatable way can be invaluable resources. They transform complex topics into understandable nuggets of information. Imagine learning about stock markets through a podcast that compares them to a giant supermarket, where instead of buying groceries, people buy and sell pieces of companies. This not only makes the concept more digestable but also quite fascinating. By integrating these resources into their daily or weekly routines, teens can develop a habit of staying informed, which will benefit them throughout their lives.

Now, onto the treasure trove of resources that can help expand their financial knowledge. There's a whole world of books, websites, and apps designed with young learners in mind. For starters, consider books that tackle money management basics or investing fundamentals. Websites like Investopedia, while more advanced, offer clear explanations and tutorials on a wide range of financial topics. For a more interactive learning experience, financial literacy apps can provide engaging ways to practice money management through simulations and games. These resources not only enhance their understanding but also make learning about finances a lot more engaging. Think of it as adding tools to their financial toolkit—each book, each website, each app helps them build skills that turn them into savvy financial navigators.

Discussing the ongoing need for financial education is crucial. It's not just about learning to budget or understanding how to save—financial education is about developing a mindset that embraces continuous learning. The financial world is always evolving, and staying educated is key to navigating it successfully. It's like being on a boat; to keep sailing smoothly, you need to adjust your sails as the wind changes. Financial education equips teens with the ability to make informed decisions, think critically about money matters, and adapt to new financial landscapes as they grow.

Engaging with financial professionals can take this learning to the next level. Encourage your teens to attend workshops or seminars. Many banks and financial institutions offer sessions tailored to young people, covering topics from basic budgeting to investing. These sessions are not just informational but also provide a platform to ask questions and interact with experts. It's a chance to demystify the financial world and see that behind those intimidating terms and concepts are opportunities waiting to be grasped. Moreover, these interactions can inspire them to explore finance as a career or deepen their personal financial knowledge.

By staying informed, utilizing educational resources, understanding the importance of continuous financial education, and engaging with professionals, teens are not just preparing to manage their finances effectively—they are setting themselves up to thrive in a world where financial acumen can open doors to opportunities and provide security and prosperity.

Vision Boarding for Financial Goals: A Creative Approach

Let's talk about a fun, artsy way to bring those financial dreams out of the clouds and down to your living room floor—creating a vision board. Picture this: a big, bright board plastered with images of the things you and your kids dream about, whether it's a bike, a trip to Disneyland, or that fancy science camp. A vision board is like your family's financial wishlist turned into a colorful collage, and it's not just for fun—it's a powerful tool to make financial goals more tangible and visually motivating.

So, how do you start this creative adventure? First, gather your supplies—magazines, markers, stickers, glue, and a big piece of poster board. Invite the kids to cut out pictures that represent their financial goals. It could be images of places they want to visit, items they wish to buy, or activities they want to save for. As they choose each image, chat about what these goals mean to them and why they're important. This is a great way to dive deeper into their values and aspirations, turning the activity into a meaningful conversation about priorities and dreams. Before you place the images on the board, have you and your child hold the images between your closed palms, close your eyes and imagine how the goals can be achieved; what your life will look like once they are achieved; how you feel about each of these images as if they were real.

Next, as you all start placing these images on the board, discuss setting a mix of short and long-term goals. Maybe the short-term goal is saving for a new video game in the next few months, while a long-term goal could be saving for college. For each goal, talk about the steps needed to achieve them, like setting aside a certain amount of allowance each week or doing extra chores for extra cash. This part of the process helps kids understand that big dreams aren't that far out of reach—they just require planning and patience. The act of physically placing these goals on a board also breaks down the abstract concept of financial planning into a concrete, visual format that's easier for kids to grasp and get excited about. DO NOT USE pre-cutouts or images supplied by others for convenience. The act of searching for the images; cutting them out; and choosing only what's best for you (or your child's best) and not what some stranger provided, allows only YOUR intent to be imbued within them. Someone else supplying pre-cutouts or previously chosen examples contains THEIR intent. Since it is their intent on making money by supplying you with images is self-fulfilling. Just remember, INTENT rules the world. Just ask Oprah Winfrey.

Now, let's explore the power of visualization. There's something almost magical about seeing your goals laid out in front of you. It makes the abstract tangible and the impossible suddenly possible. Explain to your kids how athletes use visualization to improve performance, imagining themselves winning races or scoring goals. In the same way, seeing their financial goals every day on a vision board can enhance their motivation and commitment to achieving them. It's like having a daily reminder of what they're working towards, keeping their financial aspirations clear and focused amidst the distractions of daily life.

Lastly, just like any good strategy, a vision board needs to be reviewed and updated periodically. Set a fun family ritual, maybe every six months or so, to review the board. Celebrate the goals you've achieved, and if some goals no longer resonate or if new dreams have emerged, update the board to reflect these changes. DO NOT DESTROY the board if it is no longer current. Simply roll it up, rubber band it, and put in the top of a closet for review years later to see how much you have achieved. This not only keeps the vision board dynamic and relevant but also teaches an important lesson about adaptability and growth. Goals can change, and that's perfectly okay—it's all part of the journey in managing finances and navigating life's many aspirations.

By making a vision board, you're not just crafting a pretty collage; you're building a visual and motivational tool that brings financial goals to life. It's a way to bond with your kids over shared dreams and teach them the value of planning, perseverance, and adaptability in a fun, engaging way. Dollar Tree has cheap white boards. Or shop around. So, why not make this weekend a vision board party? Turn up the music, bring out the craft supplies, and let the dreams—and the glue—flow!

Financial Independence for Teens: Early Steps

Stepping into the arena of financial independence can be a bit like learning to ride a bike—wobbly at first, maybe a few bumps along the way, but oh, the freedom once you get the hang of it! For teens, grasping this freedom not only boosts their confidence but sets a solid foundation for their future. So, let's kick-start this adventure by defining what financial independence really means for a teenager. It's not just about making money; it's about making decisions—the kind that align with personal goals and real-world needs. It's about being able to meet your expenses on your own, understanding how to manage those dollars wisely, and planning ahead for bigger dreams. This kind of independence is a powerful step toward adulthood, and believe me, it's as exciting as getting the keys to your first car.

Now, diving into the skills for earning money—these are your tools, your must-haves in your financial toolkit. Time management tops this list. It's a golden skill that helps balance school, a part-time job, and personal life. Encourage your teens to create a schedule that includes time for work, study, and play—yes, downtime is crucial too! Work ethic is another cornerstone. Whether it's flipping burgers, tutoring, or starting a garage band, approaching any job with dedication and responsibility speaks volumes. It builds character and reputation, and let's be honest, a solid work ethic opens doors, from landing better job opportunities to earning recommendations for college or future careers.

Managing personal finances is like being the captain of your own ship, steering through budgets, savings, and spending without hitting the rocks. Start with the basics: using a bank account effectively. Teach them to monitor their account regularly, understand fees, and use banking apps to track their spending. Next up, budgeting—this isn't just about keeping tabs on what you spend. It's about making informed choices that align with your goals. Show them how to set up a simple budget, categorize their expenses, and adjust as they go. It's thrilling to see your planning pay off, whether it's saving up for a concert ticket or managing daily expenses.

Planning for future expenses is where the thrill of financial independence really kicks in. It's about looking ahead, whether it's for college, travel, or a major purchase like a car. Start these conversations early. What are their dreams and goals? Map out what it might cost to achieve these dreams and strategize on how to get there. This might include setting up a dedicated savings account for college or a travel fund. Discuss the importance of making sacrifices now (like skipping that extra coffee) to reap bigger rewards later. This kind of forward-thinking is crucial; it turns abstract future needs into concrete goals they can work towards, instilling a sense of purpose in their savings efforts.

Tackling financial independence is not just about making money or learning to budget. It's about crafting a lifestyle that values responsibility, foresight, and smart financial decisions. It's about setting the stage now for the kind of life they want to lead. And let's face it, watching your teens take these steps independently is incredibly rewarding. So, as they start this exciting chapter, remind them that every financial decision is a step towards their independence, a badge of their growing maturity and freedom. What could be more exhilarating than that?

Celebrating Financial Successes: Rewarding Smart Money Choices

Imagine this: after months of diligent saving, your child finally hits their goal. Maybe they've saved enough for that special skateboard, or perhaps they've stashed away a hefty sum for a future college fund. This isn't just a win; it's a milestone! And like any significant accomplishment, it deserves a proper celebration. Recognizing and rewarding these financial milestones not only boosts morale but also reinforces the positive behaviors that got them there in the first place.

Let's explore how you can make financial successes a big deal and an inspiring lesson for your kids.

Recognizing Achievements

Celebrating financial milestones starts with recognition. It's important to acknowledge the effort and discipline it took to reach financial goals. This could be as simple as a congratulatory hug and words of praise, or as festive as a family dinner where the achiever picks the menu. Recognizing these achievements gives your child a sense of accomplishment and pride, reinforcing the value of setting and sticking to financial goals. It turns abstract concepts like saving and budgeting into tangible rewards that they can see and enjoy. Moreover, this celebration can become a teachable moment, highlighting the strategies that worked well and discussing how these can be applied to future financial goals. It's about creating a cycle of positive reinforcement that motivates continued effort and improvement.

Rewards that Reinforce Good Behavior

Choosing the right rewards is crucial—they should celebrate the achievement without contradicting the lessons of good financial management. For instance, if your child has saved diligently, a money-based reward isn't the only option. Non-monetary rewards, such as an extra hour of video games, a day trip, or a special one-on-one day with a parent, can be just as exciting. These rewards not only reinforce good behavior but also encourage a healthy balance between saving for the future and enjoying the present. It's about showing that financial responsibility isn't just about accumulation but also about using financial resources wisely to enhance life's joyous moments.

Sharing Success Stories

Encourage your child to share their success story with friends or family members. This could be at a family gathering, over a casual dinner, or during a chat with friends. Sharing not only allows them to bask in their achievement but also serves to inspire others. It turns their success into a narrative that can motivate peers and siblings to embark on their own financial saving adventures. Moreover, discussing their journey opens the floor to advice from others, perhaps drawing on the broader experiences of adults in the family or the fresh perspectives of their peers. This communal sharing of stories creates a supportive environment where financial wisdom is passed around and celebrated, much like cherished family recipes.

Reflecting on the Journey

Finally, take a moment to reflect on the journey. Sit down with your child and discuss what they learned from the experience. Which strategies worked best? What would they do differently next time? Reflection is a powerful tool for growth. It allows your child to pause and critically assess their financial decisions, understanding both their strengths and areas for improvement. This introspection ensures that each financial goal reached is a stepping stone to greater financial wisdom and confidence.

By making a big deal out of reaching financial milestones, you're not just celebrating dollars and cents; you're applauding the persistence, planning, and discipline that achieving these goals requires. It turns each financial success into a cornerstone for future endeavors, reinforcing the notion that smart money management opens the doors to both immediate rewards and long-term well-being.

As we wrap up this chapter on celebrating financial successes, it's clear that the journey through smart money management is not just about reaching destinations but also about appreciating the steps along the way. Each goal achieved, each lesson learned, and each story shared weaves into the larger tapestry of financial literacy and independence. As we continue to explore the realms of money management in the following chapters, let's carry forward the spirit of celebration, learning, and growth, ensuring that these financial lessons leave a lasting impact. Onward to our next adventure, where we'll delve deeper into the strategies that make for wise financial planning and robust economic understanding.

<u>**Conclusion**</u>

Well, my friends, we've been on quite the adventure together, haven't we? From digging into the cozy corners of money basics, sailing through the strategies of smart money management, climbing the heights of growing our pennies through investments, to surfing the waves in the vast ocean of digital finance—we've covered a lot of ground! We've built a sturdy bridge from understanding the nitty-gritty of everyday money dealings to preparing for a financially savvy future. And what a ride it's been!

Remember, starting this journey early isn't just a nice-to-have; it's a game changer. The seeds we've planted here—those foundational concepts of budgeting, saving, and making thoughtful spending choices—are going to grow into mighty trees of financial wisdom as you and your young ones continue to nurture them.

This book isn't just a bunch of facts and figures; we've tried to stitch in those essential life skills with the nitty-gritty of finances. It's all about making those numbers relatable, turning abstract ideas into fun, interactive learning experiences with games, projects, and a sprinkle of real-life magic. We've designed each activity to not just teach but to inspire curiosity and confidence, whether it's through setting up a lemonade stand or planning a family budget.

And let's talk about inclusivity. We've woven a rich tapestry that includes everyone, recognizing that while the value of money is universal, each of us may dance to a slightly different financial tune due to our unique backgrounds and perspectives. This book aims to resonate with everyone, no matter where you come from or what your money story is.

Now, don't let this be the end. Oh no, let's keep this curiosity burning bright! The financial landscape is always changing, and staying informed is staying empowered. Keep exploring, keep learning, and why not share this newfound knowledge? Talk about it at dinner tables, during car rides, or while waiting in the school pick-up line. Sharing not only reinforces what you've learned but also spreads the wisdom further into your community.

So, what's next? How about we take some of this book's lessons and put them into action right away? Maybe start by helping your kids set up their first budget, or plan out a saving strategy for that cool new bike or video game they've been eyeing. Dive into one of the activities we explored and make it a fun weekend project.

And as you step forward, remember, managing money is indeed a lifelong journey. There will be ups, downs, and a few loop-the-loops along the way. But with the toolkit you now have, I have every confidence that you're well-prepared to face those challenges head-on. You're not just saving money; you're building a future. And that's pretty amazing!

My hope, my big dream, is that this book lights a spark—a spark that burns brightly in the young minds of your children, guiding them towards making smart, informed, and confident financial choices. Here's to a future where they not only manage their finances wisely but do so with joy and a deep understanding of how money can be a tool for good in their hands.

Thank you for joining me on this incredible journey. Keep flipping those pages, keep asking questions, and let's keep growing richer in every sense of the word. Happy saving, spending, and sharing, everyone! Here's to a financially savvy future, crafted with love, laughter, and a whole lot of learning. Cheers!

References

◇ Teaching Kids About Money: An Age-by-Age Guide https://www.parents.com/parenting/money/family-finances/teaching-kids-about-money-an-age-by-age-guide/

◇ Money and Finance: History of Money https://www.ducksters.com/money/history_of_money.php

◇ How to teach kids about Money & Budgeting (Simple Game)   https://theceokid.com/how-to-teach-kids-about-budgeting-simple-game/

◇ Explaining Needs vs. Wants to Your Child (Without ... https://www.gohenry.com/us/blog/financial-education/explaining-needs-vs-wants-to-your-child-without-overwhelming-them

◇ Budgeting for kids: Fun ways to teach budgeting to kids https://www.gohenry.com/us/blog/financial-education/budgeting-for-kids-fun-ways-to-teach-budgeting-to-kids

◇ Best Savings Accounts for Kids and Teens for July 2024— ...   https://www.investopedia.com/best-savings-accounts-for-kids-5179494

⬦ Teaching children about money - Canada.ca
https://www.canada.ca/en/financial-consumer-agency/
services/teaching-children-
money.html#:~:text=Make%20learning%20about%20saving%20fun,wh

⬦ How to Help Kids and Teens Avoid Impulse Buying
https://www.mydoh.ca/learn/blog/lifestyle/how-to-help-
kids-and-teens-avoid-impulse-buying/

⬦ Teach Kids About Money: Financial Literacy For Kids
https://www.tiaa.org/public/learn/life-milestones/
teaching-kids-about-money

⬦ Simple Interest vs. Compound Interest: What's the ...
https://www.investopedia.com/ask/answers/042315/
what-difference-between-compounding-interest-and-
simple-interest.asp

⬦ Best investment accounts for kids 2024
https://www.usatoday.com/money/blueprint/investing/
best-investment-accounts-for-kids/

⬦ How to Teach Your Kids About Financial Goals
https://www.linkedin.com/pulse/how-teach-your-kids-
financial-goals-junio-smart-card-alcqc

⬦ The Best Children's Financial Literacy Apps for 2023
https://moonpreneur.com/blog/children-financial-
literacy-app/

⬦ How Online Banking Works: A Beginner's Guide
https://www.missionfed.com/news-stories/how-online-
banking-works-a-beginners-guide/

◇ A Guide to Online Shopping Safety for Kids - Bark https://www.bark.us/blog/online-shopping-safety/

◇ Explaining cryptocurrency to children - MoneySense https://natwest.mymoneysense.com/parents/articles/how-to-explain-cryptocurrency-to-children/

◇ How to Help Kids Learn to Love Giving https://greatergood.berkeley.edu/article/item/how_to_help_kids_learn_to_love_giving

◇ What Is Tax? - Lesson for Kids - Study.com https://study.com/academy/lesson/what-is-tax-lesson-for-kids.html#:~:text=Lesson%20Summary-,Taxes%20are%20ways%20that%20the%20government%20can%20

◇ How Parents Can Educate Their Kids About Financial Scams https://www.todaysparent.com/family/parenting/how-to-educate-kids-about-financial-scams/

◇ What is Ethical Consumption? Decisions for a Better Planet https://www.transformationholdings.com/climate-change/ethical-consumption/

◇ 18 Fun Money Activities for Kids https://www.gohenry.com/us/blog/financial-education/18-fun-money-activities-for-kids

◇ The complete guide to entrepreneurship for kids https://www.gohenry.com/us/blog/money-management/the-gohenry-guide-to-entrepreneurship

◇ Online Games and Apps That Teach Kids About Money https://dfi.wa.gov/financial-education/educators/online-games-and-apps

◇ The role of banknotes in promoting national identity and … https://www.citech.com/the-role-of-banknotes-in-promoting-national-identity-and-culture/

◇ How to Help Kids and Teens Avoid Impulse Buying https://www.mydoh.ca/learn/blog/lifestyle/how-to-help-kids-and-teens-avoid-impulse-buying/

◇ Budgeting for kids: Fun ways to teach budgeting to kids https://www.gohenry.com/us/blog/financial-education/budgeting-for-kids-fun-ways-to-teach-budgeting-to-kids

◇ Teaching Kids About Money: 7 Mistakes to Avoid https://www.americanheritagecu.org/about-us/american-heritage-and-the-community/blog/moneyblog/2023/04/13/teaching-kids-about-money-7-mistakes-to-avoid#:~:text=Allow%20your%20child%20to%20make,better%20choic

◇ 38 Best Fundraising Ideas for Kids in 2023 https://www.classy.org/blog/fundraising-ideas-for-kids/

◇ 21 Financial Literacy Games to Make Learning Fun - OppU https://www.opploans.com/oppu/financial-literacy/games-financial-literacy/

◇ How to Teach Kids Budgeting: A Simple Guide for Parents https://www.primewayfcu.com/blog/teach-kids-budgeting-skills

◇ Benefits of a Teenager Getting a Job https://www.webmd.com/parenting/benefits-of-a-teenager-getting-a-job

◇ How to create a financial goals vision board that works … https://financialbestlife.com/creating-a-vision-board/

Don't miss out!

Visit the website below and you can sign up to receive emails whenever Jordan Rivers publishes a new book. There's no charge and no obligation.

https://books2read.com/r/B-A-YHHHB-JSYWD

BOOKS2READ

Connecting independent readers to independent writers.

Also by Jordan Rivers

Hunky Nerd Series
Hunky Nerd 1 & 2

Standalone
A Duchess's Redemption
Víspera de brujas
Witches' Eve
The Five Suitors
Empowered Survival: A Comprehensive Guide For Women
The Weekend Fisherman's Cookbook
Easy Fitness for Seniors
High Desert
How to Train for the Combine
Alto Desierto
Supervivencia Empoderada: ung guia completa para mujeres
The Hunky Nerd Collection
Kids and money: Fast track your kids for a practical life